The Naked Manager

How to Build Open Relationships at Work

Here's what others say about *The Naked Manager*:

Eileen approaches the subject of effective management with a simplicity that I found very appropriate. She's made it clear that managers at all levels can influence their environments by their own thoughts, actions, reactions and responses. We resist the simple "naked" truths about ourselves and others in our personal lives and in our organizations, yet awakening and responding to these very truths is what provides the success and fulfillment we all seek. Raising that awareness is a great service to managers and all who work with them. I enjoyed reading this book and applaud Eileen's efforts.

> Margaret M. Urquhart
> President
> Lowes Foods

A lot of management books you read are forgotten after a week. This is the kind of book that will stay with people. It is down to earth and concrete. Eileen's honest style and her use of humor are refreshingly disarming.

> Debbie Morris
> Human Resource Director
> Northern Telecom

More than ever it is important to have honest relationships in the workplace. *The Naked Manager* will help you do just that.

> Wally Amos
> Founder, Famous Amos Cookies
> Author, *Watermelon Magic:*
> *Seeds of Wisdom, Slice of Life*

I thoroughly enjoyed reading this refreshing book. *The Naked Manager* helps today's managers make larger sense of critical human dynamics and the role they play in the turbulent corporate game. This is management 2000 and beyond!

> Jillian Austin
> Director, US Relations
> The Americas Cup

Reading *The Naked Manager* will enhance your communication style and your ability to interact effectively with colleagues. I found the book quite revealing and look forward to working with naked managers in the future.

> Jim McCann
> Chief Executive Officer
> 1-800-FLOWERS

The Naked Manager

How to Build Open Relationships at Work

Eileen Dowse

Oakhill Press
Greensboro, North Carolina

This publication is designed to provide accurate and authoritative information in regard to the subject matter covered. It is sold with the understanding that the publisher is not engaged in rendering legal, accounting, or other professional service. If legal advice or other expert assistance is required, the services of a competent professional person should be sought. *From a Declaration of Principles jointly adopted by a committee of the American Bar Association and a committee of Publishers.*

10   9   8   7   6   5   4   3   2   1

Library of Congress Cataloging in Publication Data

Dowse, Eileen., 1958–
     The naked manager : how to build open relationships at work / Eileen Dowse
          p. cm.
     Includes bibliographical references and index.
     ISBN 1-886939-24-1 (pbk.)
     1. Psychology, Industrial.   2. Management.   I. Title.
HF5548.8.D67   1998
     158.7—dc21   98-19059
                                                              CIP

Contents

Dedicated to my husband David,
a wonderful partner, who always understands that I
need to have a paper and pen handy, wherever I go.

And to my children,
whose spectacular spirits help to remind me how
important humor is in life.

Introduction

Naked managers achieve results. They move on a path toward success by being authentic and insightful. To determine if you are a naked manager, rate yourself on the following statements.

1. **I have the resources I need to do a good job.**
   strongly agree   agree   disagree   strongly disagree

2. **My work represents my beliefs.**
   strongly agree   agree   disagree   strongly disagree

3. **People in my organization know what I represent.**
   strongly agree   agree   disagree   strongly disagree

4. **I am challenged by new ideas and approaches.**
   strongly agree   agree   disagree   strongly disagree

5. **I have unique talents that I am using to benefit my work.**
   strongly agree   agree   disagree   strongly disagree

6. **I know that people understand what I'm saying.**
   strongly agree   agree   disagree   strongly disagree

7. **I act on my hunches.**
   strongly agree   agree   disagree   strongly disagree

8. **I consistently work with integrity as my guide.**
   strongly agree   agree   disagree   strongly disagree

If you answered "strongly agree" to all seven statements, you can be sure that you are well on the way to being a naked manager. If not, this book offers you the insights for reaching that goal.

The Naked Manager is based on solutions I have developed during 20 years of working with the same problems again and again—problems that stop people in business from achieving success and gratification from their work."

The creation of this book began early one morning as I was getting ready to coach a corporate client through a management crisis. I had just gotten out of the shower, when I stopped and stared at my naked reflection in the mirror. The answer I had been looking for to help troubled managers emerged right in front of me. I stood there naked, with no covering to hide under. I was there totally, visibly—my blemishes, my beauties, and more of my blemishes.

It is not very much fun to stand gawking at ourselves in the buff. Quite often we are disappointed with what we see and spend more time disliking the truth than accepting and working with it. Yet there I was looking at myself, buck naked, in front of the mirror that morning, viewing the perfect metaphor for my work. By putting on clothes or veils, we can cover up our flaws, divert attention to ourselves, or create false pictures of what lies below. Samuel Butler wrote, "Our minds want clothes as much as our bodies."[1]

It is not easy to look in a mirror and accept what you see. It is hard to say, "This is me. This is what I've got. This is what I have to work with!" It is difficult to get naked. I experienced it, and I know my clients experience it in their careers. At the most basic level, nakedness means removing all that is superfluous and dispensable and acknowledging a state of nature. Being comfortable with our nakedness means approaching and working with the blemishes and the beauties we possess. We all start out naked and through life's experiences we, metaphorically and figuratively, clothe ourselves for protection.

Typically by the time I am called in to help, my clients are in crisis. The first thing I notice when I speak with managers is how many protective layers they have created between themselves and their employees. When I investigate the issues facing them more thoroughly, I recognize that those same distancing layers have often come between the managers' true selves and their workplace personas. What this means is that they are working on a shallow level.

Managers and companies spend a great deal of energy putting on layers while they ignore what lies below. What managers often neglect is harnessing the power that is present in themselves and their co-workers, the power that is there naturally. Being naked means taking off the layers and veils and revealing the core. And the core is where true power lies.

The success I have had in coaching my clients has always come from helping them get naked and deal with issues at the core level. Whenever managers shed those protective layers and help others do the same, they create opportunities for working more effectively, decreasing stress, and increasing productivity and employee performance.

It doesn't matter who you manage—your staff, your children, or your family. The simple fact is that it is uncomfortable when people get emotionally or physically naked. That morning in front of the mirror, experiencing discomfort with my nakedness, I realized that I, like many managers, was confronted with the same four issues.

1. Feeling of vulnerability. Many people think that if you tell too much about yourself, the chance of attack, revenge, or bribery increases. They are afraid of being embarrassed publicly. I'm not talking about the fear you have when toilet paper is hanging off your shoe or, even worse, your waistband. I'm talking about the fear of exposing your internal thought processes and styles. We don't want people to know our quirks, styles, or secrets, lest we be considered different from others.

2. Fear of being valued. You have chosen your profession because you believe (and want others to believe!) you have some quality to bring to the position. You also have some need to be recognized for your endeavors. People want to feel valued, but resist opening up and talking about what they need. They either fear the response they might get, or they devalue their own worth and simply don't ask.

3. Worry about being perceived as different. Our culture is not like a nudist colony. People in general don't behave as though they value the freedom to be free, unique, and natural. We are more concerned with images and outer layers. As a society we have a tough time getting past them. We don't focus on the layer below the surface, the layer that *really* makes up the person.

4. Lack of self awareness. It is uncommon for individuals to be educated about knowing themselves, their styles, and their behavior. People assume managers know who they are and have the confidence to do the job. It is difficult to be comfortable and confident, if you don't know yourself in your entirety.

The Naked Manager will show you how to be yourself, in all your glory. It will recommend ways to spend your time using your natural abilities and talents to manage and guide others. The information in this book will offer approaches for stripping the cover-up and phoniness we clothe ourselves in, the obstructions that get in the way of effectiveness. It is not my intention that you go out and get arrested for indecent exposure. That is why I did not create a chapter entitled "Birthday Suits . . . Dress for Success!" This book is not about getting *physically* naked, but about recognizing your true unedited self and gaining the strength and confidence to manage the day-to-day issues that face you in your role.

The purpose of this book is to help you, become comfortable to be, to manage without fear. If you think managing is always comfortable, it's not. If you think being naked all the time is comfortable, it's not. What is important is to be comfortable being uncomfortable.

In 20 years of working with managers I have discovered eight *Bare* Essentials—eight ways to reach your naked self. These have become the eight chapters of this book and are directly related to the Naked Manager Quiz. Each addresses ways to improve your awareness and performance as a manager.

The Eight Bare Essentials

1. **Sagging with Gravity:** *The need for support systems*

2. **Elective Surgery**: *Taking the organ out of organizations* (Problems caused by change . . . and their solutions)

3. **Exposing Yourself:** *Being au naturel from all angles* (Conveying your truths in a way people can hear)

4. **Big Buts:** *Positive attitudes and creative minds* (Encouraging creativity and innovation)

5. **Birthmarks**: *Using uniqueness to your advantage*

6. **From Ear to Ear:** *Communicating accurately*

7. **Natural Instincts:** *Using your intuition*

8. **That's the Spirit:** *Spirituality in the workplace*

Managers all over the world struggle with these issues. I have surveyed leaders from Australia, France, Canada, England, and the United States to provide even more information on what managers face today. I have asked them for their solutions and approaches to these dilemmas. At the end of each chapter, I will give a summary of these common thoughts in a section entitled *Solutions from the collective wisdom.* I encourage you to contact me with insights that surface as you shed your own layers. Together we can discover ways for all managers to become more effective and complete because of their nakedness.

1

What's the Big Deal about Nakedness?

Becoming a Naked Manager

The first time I was conscious of feeling naked and vulnerable was at the ripe old age of 25. I was in the process of giving birth to my first son. Until that point I had felt in control of how I wanted my nakedness to be perceived by others. Then, at 10 cm dilated, my intimate partner and lifelong friend, my husband, at my side, we entered the delivery room filled with strangers, coaches, and professionals. These would be the players for the next 36 hours. I knew as part of this group I played a key role in the outcome. Each person present was needed for the unique skills and talents he or she brought to the process. I felt vulnerable, out of control, anxious, frightened, and by this point, passionate to get the task completed. I was mentally and partially physically naked as my "a-que-tra-ments" (as my mother calls them) were open to the world.

I remember entering the delivery room feeling apprehensive and uncomfortable about being the focal point for making things happen. Two hours into the delivery process, my view of nakedness and vulnerability had changed. The direction of focus was now on the task at hand, not on what people thought about me. I was no longer bogged down with concerns for protecting my superficial and subliminal self. I put all my energy into my mission and purpose. I chose *not* to spend energy on thoughts that would hinder the completion of this project. My focal point became centered on making things happen and welcoming anyone around me to join in.

With a human and honest approach I communicated my standpoint and confirmed with the doctors and staff their thoughts on the situation. Together, this group of people on June 15, 1983, helped create an entity. It required all of us working together for the final result to occur.

Thinking back on the events of that day, I realize that feeling vulnerable only hinders the creation process. Attitude is pivotal to managing events. Drive, spirit, and strong determination are the attributes needed for making things happen. For me, these traits helped produce a 10 pound, 7 ounce baby boy, brought into the world through natural childbirth.

This process of becoming a naked manager is analogous to the birthing process. Becoming mentally naked means being conscious of your role in the final outcome. Like giving birth, becoming a naked manager is a mind shift toward being comfortable with vulnerability and using humanness to your advantage. This shift expands on those traditional management styles of planning, organizing, and controlling. It broadens the scope to include leadership of performance and incorporates:

- *being comfortable* functioning in an open and honest fashion

- *maintaining* an authentic and uncorrupted management style

- *possessing* confidence to value yours and others contributions

- *disclosing* who you really are, to build and increase levels of trust

- *recognizing* that lamination in leadership discredits competencies

Managers today are under tremendous pressure to make things happen. As organizations flatten, people are learning that the need to become more real and less covert is critical to the effective management of people. It is time for managers to get naked and deliver.

By using the naked manager approach you can:

- focus on vitality and higher results
  —creating freedom to encourage optimum potential

- build trust and collaboration
  —reinforcing accountability and relationships

- increase personal and employee satisfaction
  —developing high levels of respect, morale, and integrity

- generate active resolution to problems
  —allowing issues to surface and solutions to be created

- direct the focus toward group synergy
  —moving from superficial association to amalgamation

- promote insights to anticipating problems before they occur
  —taking a preventative approach to leading

You have the ability to make things happen and to transform the way you achieve results. How will you choose to use your power? I recommend you remove the barriers that restrict you and work from a position of strength. The decision to become a naked manager is up to you. It always has been.

Solutions from the collective wisdom

- Don't be afraid to open up, it could be your most powerful tool.
- Show your human side, get out there and take risks, that's the way to use the power of relationships.
- When you're comfortable with yourself, the rest of work is a lot easier.
- Negative perceptions stifle success, give yourself credit for believing you can do the job. If you don't believe it, why should anyone else?
- Change the way you look at things, if everyone was acting vulnerable and different it would be the norm, the way you have to behave is your choice.
- Things are always going to change, accept the fact, bite the bullet, and go for it.
- Sitting, doing nothing, gets you nothing. Go after what you want. You can make it happen. Believe in yourself.
- When you start to have a good relationship with your employees you take all the guesswork out of getting the information you need from them.
- Using your heart is just as important as using your head.
- When I'm honest my stress level decreases.

2

Sagging with Gravity
The Need for Support Systems

As we age, gravity convinces our body parts to head south. The solution to this biological dilemma is a well-balanced support system. Toning the abdominal muscles can do wonders. Another approach is to find external support devices to hold things in place and help stop the sagging.

Managers often sag when the demands and expectations of everyday life push against them. As in life, the best business solution for battling this force is to rely on your support system, the network of people you've chosen to help you hold up all those important parts that begin to droop with pressure. If you wonder, "What support system?" then read on. Managers need to have a support system, a network to help them deal with the multitude of issues that challenge them each day.

The following is a simple technique for analyzing your current support system.

Instructions:
1. **Review** the definitions of support system individuals.
2. **Write** the names of people you know who fit the appropriate description in the circles on the support system diagram on page 14.
   - If the person you know fits into more than one category, put him or her in as many categories for which he or she qualifies.
   - If you can't think of someone for a particular circle, leave it blank.
   - If you think you are the best match for that circle, put your name in.

Support System Definitions

MENTORS: (*Use these people for direction*) Mentors help with clarity and are essential when you are confused about the future. Their wealth of experiential and professional knowledge is there for you to observe and emulate. They are people with whom you can brainstorm about accomplishing your goals. They are a good benchmark.

FOREVER FRIENDS: *(Use these people for relief)* Forever Friends are the people you can depend on in a crisis. There is no end to their willingness to help "any time." They can deal with any challenge and offer all kinds of assistance. A Forever Friend is someone you can call at 3:00 a.m. without feeling guilty.

CONTENDERS: *(Use these people for opposition)* Contenders will disagree and challenge your thinking to help you out of the tunnel vision rut. They energize and promote clear thinking by continually asking you to justify your thoughts and opinions.

CONNECTORS: *(Use these people for linkups)* Connectors can guide you in the right direction. They know the people to contact and the places for locating things to help you accomplish your task.

BUDDIES: *(Use these people for fun times)* Buddies are people you can share similar interests and activities with. You can call them any time to share your joyous moments. You can walk, sail, cycle, or hang out with Buddies. These are the individuals who give you the chance to get out and enjoy life.

PARTNERS: *(Use these people for task accomplishment)* Partners are people with whom you can accomplish tasks because of your complementary styles and similar values. Together you and your Partner make the workload easier and more bearable.

SUPPORT SYSTEMS

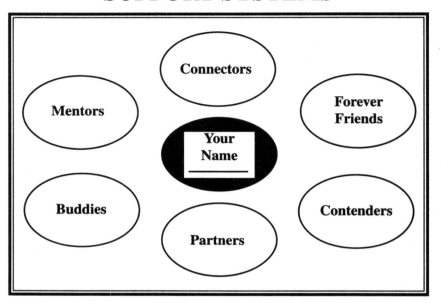

Mentors . . . observe, emulate, and share experience and knowledge

Forever Friends . . . can be depended on in a crisis; they will help whenever you need them

Contenders . . . challenge your thinking and cause you to focus more clearly on issues

Connectors . . . link you to people, places, things, and ideas that you need

Buddies . . . share similar interests and celebrate your successes

Partners . . . complement and enhance your styles and viewpoints

Support System

Analysis Questions

After completing this exercise, step back and contemplate the final results. Ask yourself the following questions.

1. Do you have all the circles filled in? If you don't, what support systems are missing for you?

2. Are all your categories filled with people who live more than 50 miles away? If so, how can they actively support you? Are the people in your support system easily accessible? (Long-distance support systems aren't always the most helpful and useful.)

3. Do you have different people's names in each category or are you your own support system? (As humans we need several people to help us deal with the issues we face each day. Your support system circles should have a variety of people's names in them.)

4. Does one person's name appear in all the categories? Are you overburdening that resource and potentially causing him or her to burn out? Have you placed all your eggs in one basket? (If something happens to that one person, you're left without a support network.)

If each circle is filled in with a different name, this support system theory implies:

- you are willing to ask for help

- you are open to comments and feedback

- your sagging parts have support

- you have a balanced network to help you in difficult situations

Remember, sometimes feedback and the truth from a support system is hard to swallow and accept. On the other hand, remember that you are the person who is responsible for your actions. Anyone can give recommendations or comfort, but you are the one that has to implement it and live with it. It is all a matter of keeping things in perspective and making decisions based on your style, needs, and resources. *You* are the naked one with sagging parts; *you* get to choose which approach will work best.

As a manager, don't be naked and vulnerable alone. When you are working under pressure, with the gravitational forces pulling you down, it is important to be able to access your support system to keep you balanced and successful. The goal for a naked manager is to create a well-balanced network and support system to help effectively deal with all the situations arising from your role.

Support systems require care and maintenance in turn. It is amazing how even the smallest events can affect a support network.

This lesson came home to a friend of mine named Scott. He was going to meet and work with another sales rep, someone who was part of his support network. Although Scott had never met this individual in person, they had arranged by phone to meet at a restaurant. They would talk there for a while, then get into one car and drive together to the customer with plans of making a sale. Scott knew it was important to make a good impression on this new colleague. There was a thought that this individual could be a mentor for Scott. He had heard that this person had a great deal of experience and wisdom and if the two of them could work well together, there was money to be made and deals to be had. Good impressions were paramount, and using this support system could help make the sale of lifetime. The pressure was on and the potential was great.

On this particular day Scott was having one of those hectic mornings and he was running late for this important meeting. Trying to get to the restaurant quickly, he approached the on-ramp and merged into the highway traffic. As he got onto the highway, he accidentally cut off the driver behind him. He felt awful. It was a mistake. There was no damage done, or at least none to the vehicles. The driver of the other car was a little more than annoyed. He drove up beside Scott and, at 65 miles an hour, flipped him the finger while mouthing some angry words through the passenger window. Scott figured, fine, I deserve it, I made a mistake, I'm sorry.

But, it didn't end there. The driver of the other car sped forward and cut Scott off. That was it. The battle had begun! Scott accepted being flipped off, but he *didn't* accept intentionally being cut off. The two drivers now drove down the highway side by side, maneuvering for position. They made gestures to each other and yelled obscenities through their car windows.

Scott figured the game was over as he got off at the exit for the restaurant. Yet, the other driver got off at the same exit. He was following him! Unbelievable! The gestures and motions continued on the side road. Scott drove ahead and quickly turned into the Shoney's restaurant parking lot. So did the other driver! This was too much! Scott got out of the car thinking, Great, I've got this idiot who is going to make a scene while I'm supposed to be making a good impression on this new colleague and a key individual in my network.

The other driver got out of his car, and for a brief time in the parking lot the two of them exchanged choice words face to face. It was not a pretty picture. A closing statement was made about how a body part could be used to solve the problem, and then Scott walked into Shoney's. He was already late, and this incident didn't help him feel composed and at his best. He looked around the restaurant. He didn't see anyone resembling a sales rep. He came back to the restaurant entrance and *standing there* was the other driver. Scott stopped, paused, and swallowed. He turned to the person and asked, "You're not the company rep I'm supposed to meet, are you?" It was determined that he was and now the two of them had to figure out where to go from there. It went without saying that neither of them wanted to work with the other. They decided to take separate cars to the customer. The sales meeting did not go well. They couldn't work together. It's that way even today.

You never know who might make up your support network. Choose your actions wisely.

Solutions from the collective wisdom

- Give yourself time to discuss different aspects of work with different people.
- Realize that every person can be a potential support system.
- Take the risk and ask a person to be your mentor—it can produce great results.
- Figure out the areas you need help in, and find people or training to fill those gaps.
- Work on having the resources you need available to you.
- Be flexible in your thinking and consider the perspectives of other people.
- Take the time to plan what you need.
- Surround yourself with partners and associates who can help you in your endeavors.
- Consider people from different professions to be part of your network.
- Recognize that people of all ages have insights to life and can be helpful.
- Take care of and value your network; then it will always be there for you.

3

Elective Surgery
*Taking the Organ
out of Organizations*

Words like downsizing, reengineering, layoffs, and reorganization have become part of our culture and our view of the work world. Each leads to the same thing: change. To the best of my knowledge, the only person who likes change is a wet baby; and even most babies struggle during the process. Most people resist change. They perceive it as taking the organ out of the organization. That organization can be the company, department, or individual. Organizations need organs, those parts that perform a specific function essential to the basic structure. Without organs, organizations could die. Understanding who owns the problem during a transitional time can help keep organs functional so they can keep things alive.

I like to compare the process of change to having surgery. A medical professional tells you surgery is critical for your continued well-being. You are torn. The doctor's expertise makes you inclined to accept the procedure, but you fear what it might take from you. The medical procedure begins with the information-gathering phase—medical history, current medical status. Similarly, the changing organization may begin with a needs assessment, a strategic planning session, or some method of determining the business blood type and genetic structure. Like medical evaluations, obtaining this information is critical to know so you can determine what exists before you change it.

Once the medical assessment is complete, it is time for you to prepare for surgery—or in an organization, get ready for change. When you have surgery, you trade your normal attire for a hospital gown—the one that exposes your posterior. In surgery as with organizational change, it is only natural to feel uncomfortable. In some cases you may even have a strong desire to cover your back. After all, who wants to show parts you can't even see?

The surgical procedure begins. You lie on the stretcher, complying with instructions, partially inhibited because of the effects of the numbing "stuff" you have been given prior to the operation. You find it difficult to keep your wits about you.

When an organization is in a change mode, it's also difficult to deal with the "stuff" given to you. Organizational numbness can be caused by:

- relearning new procedures

- outsourcing parts of or the entire job

- training in new methods and techniques

- less money to do the work with

- benchmarking to stay competitive

- requiring high levels of achievement and satisfaction
- value-added methods to please the customer and the higher-ups
- less people to complete the task
- assigned more work to do in less time
- merging systems and departments
- changing rules for the old game played
- goal-setting in 30-minute increments

When you wake up, whether from change or surgery, something has been removed or altered and you have been affected. Often those around you have been affected, too. During this time you might feel

- semiconscious
- worried about scarring
- afraid of being alone
- in need of support
- overwhelmed
- confused
- dependent
- alert to watch for infection
- in pain
- numb
- nauseated
- exhausted

Following surgery comes the healing process. Organizational gurus refer to this as a grieving time. It is the time to motivate and encourage people toward the new direction. Attitudes can be severely affected when an important organ has been removed. Maybe your *heart* isn't in it anymore. Or you just don't have the *guts* to do it. Perhaps you're not in the right *head* space. Or it's just a pain in the *neck*. This is when you believe the organ has been taken from your organization. It is during this organ extraction period that the manager's responsibility of motivating and encouraging becomes even more important.

After surgery many different reactions occur and not all patients respond similarly. In truth, with change or surgery your mental and physical state has been affected. It can be a time of great annoyance and discomfort, or a time for changing your perspective. Amidst change careful monitoring is needed. In this postoperative state you, and others around you, may experience:

- a *revelation* of "what is really important" for you or the organization

- *anger,* knowing this new life requires too many adjustments and you are unwilling or unable to handle it

- a *teachable moment* and view things differently for making future decisions

- *appreciation* for what you had and wish it would all return to what was

- a new *sense of caution* and look for the signs of this happening again ("once burned, twice shy")

- *gratitude* that you made it through alive and are happy just to be here

The primary challenge for the naked manager during this change process is how to approach and solve problems (pre- and postoperative). You have a responsibility for recognizing and communicating situations within the system before they become emergencies or major problems. If you are a naked manager, you may become a target for people who want you to listen, accept, and solve problems for them. They want *you* to take ownership and control of problems to relieve them of their pain and discomfort. This is why determining problem ownership is key to re-creating a better work environment.

Diagnosing Ownership

Ownership of a problem can be entrapping—and this is why clarity is crucial. Your first and most important step is to determine *who* owns the problem. Too many times I meet individuals who have a personal issue with problem ownership. They take on more problems than they need to and thereby make themselves less effective. Taking on too many "other people's problems" can take the organ out of your organization because it will be sure to suck the life out of you.

Sometimes managers own other people's problems because they cannot determine who really owns it or it is simply easier just to solve it themselves. There are cases when the problem is a case of joint ownership. And there are times when the problem is entirely the other person's. In this problem-solving roundabout, there are three distinct components: Their Problem, My Problem, and Our Problem. Each comes with a set of approaches and skills to use in order to move forward. All of them are part of the problem-solving equation as seen on the diagram "Strategies and Approaches to Problem Ownership".

Strategies and Approaches to Problem Ownership

Their Problem

- ◆ listen actively
- ◆ rephrase
- ◆ probe
- ◆ validate
- ◆ brainstorm
- ◆ coach
- ◆ clarify values
- ◆ defuse
- ◆ clarify issues

My Problem

- ◆ manage conflict
- ◆ make a decision
- ◆ take risks
- ◆ be flexible
- ◆ confront
- ◆ gather information
- ◆ create an action plan

Acknowledgment

Observable Behaviors

verbal/nonverbal clues
blaming
anger
denial
panic
impulsivity
dependence

My Problem

- ◆ involve each party
- ◆ enlist commitment
- ◆ delegate
- ◆ collaborate
- ◆ understand roles
- ◆ encourage
- ◆ facilitate
- ◆ trust

Observable Behaviors

impulsiveness
challenging
controlling
interdependency
cohesiveness
responsibility
aggression

Most managers quickly own problems and take on the burden of solving them because it might seem easier that way. While it might be easier in the short term, owning the problems of others can be hazardous to your health. Managers fall into owning others' problems because they are not aware of how to keep problems separate or how to confront and discuss the situation. If a job doesn't get done, whose problem is it? In this example, a manager could ask the following questions to establish ownership:

- "I noticed the job is not getting done. Why is that?"
  Here you are gathering information and encouraging dialogue.

- "What will it take for you to get the job done?"
  Begin generating options from the individual only.

- "What part do you want me to have in this solution?"
  Define perceptions of roles to avoid conflict caused by assumptions.

Note at no time did any of these questions imply that you, the manager, would solely take on the problem. All the questions were aimed at seeking an understanding of perspectives on the problem. Your purpose in identifying whose problem it is thus includes:

- identifying the issues

- identifying the causes

- stating your openness to assist in the creation of the solution

- establishing a relationship that does not automatically take on the problem or solution alone or by default

The questions and comments you offer are meant to allow and encourage people to identify and be part of the solution.

Imagine someone who has been assigned the responsibility for the first agenda item is late to your meeting. You could respond:

"Jamie's not here. I guess I'll take her part." (my problem)

"Jamie's not here to present. What would you like to do about this?" (our problem)

"Jamie has missed the opportunity to present and I have not received any indication of how they want to proceed on this issue." (their problem)

Naked managers bring a lot to the operating table. They can distinguish problem ownership because they are comfortable and satisfied with themselves. They don't crave control or owning all the problems. Psychologist Abraham Maslow calls this level of confidence *self-actualization.* Those who are self-actualized have satisfied their fundamental needs and understand their potential and capability. They show maturity, constructive behavior, creativity, happiness, and wisdom.

Someone at this maturity/confidence level would be described as being:

- free from unwarranted optimism or pessimism and other distortions of reality

- more tolerant of human moral or physical weaknesses and defects of character

- less judgmental of themselves and others

- spontaneous and natural in his or her behavior

- better able to comprehend true motives, emotions, abilities, and potentials

- less in need of manipulating others for selfish purposes

- less afraid of disappointment

I once shared this list with a manager. His response was, "Heck Eileen, you can achieve most of this list with an antidepressant like Prozac. Only it would be faster and easier!" I defended my theory by saying, "Reaching a contentment level without the use of chemicals allows a person to function at a natural level of comfort and authenticity for longer periods of time and with less dependency."

A person who is comfortable with his or her potentials and capabilities does not have a inherent *need* to solve other people's problems to increase his or her own sense of self. In fact, I find that the managers who are most effective are the ones who do not have an overabundance of needs. Their sense of self is intact and has been earned by experiencing and facing challenges. If you get gratification from owning others' problems, ask yourself why. Are you fixing a problem to increase your self-esteem, or are your motives more broad and are your actions doing what is best for the organization?

Their Problem

Some individuals, for a multitude of reasons, take on problems that are not their own. They solve these problems to satisfy *their own* needs or beliefs, not because it will benefit the other person. If you think as a manager you should solve others' problems, stop "shoulding" yourself. Start thinking about who owns the problem and who is going to be responsible for the consequences.

People often want to own the problem because it gives them a sense of control or value. Some people believe they are the "Problem Prime." "I'll Own It and I'll Fix It" is their motto. You can build a reputation for always owning the problem. And don't you worry, people will help, support, and encourage you in maintaining this reputation. Why? Because they won't have to take responsibility for themselves. They approach you in hopes that you will understand and side with them and ultimately do problem solving for them.

Altering these patterns begins by recognizing what problems belong solely to other people. This recognizing assumes that those who own a problem are responsible for dealing with the problem. The key here is detaching yourself from the problem and believing it is their problem. There are three important points to remember about people who are hoping you will take on the problem so they don't have to deal with it:

1. They have somehow been part of the creation of the problem, either by actions or responses.

2. They have gotten themselves entangled in it and are surfacing their fears, concerns, values, or expectations.

3. They are bothered because of *their* perception of the situation.

Often you can observe certain "I want you to own the problem" engaging behaviors. Watch and listen to people's reactions about situations. You may gain insightful clues as they weave their "please own this problem for me" magic before your very eyes. Some of the approaches you might detect are:

The Inkling: They *hint* that it's a mutual problem.
> *"I've been talking to our people, and they think this project is not going well."*
- They wait for your "I'll help to own this problem" response.

The Subliminal Message: They throw out *hidden* messages, hoping you will catch on.
> *"This is overwhelming. I just don't know what to do."* or *"Can you imagine anyone would say that to me?"*
- They wait for the "I'll save you" or "I know just what you mean" tone in your voice as you begin to comment and—whammy—you have been hooked into that problem.

Blame: They *blame* you for the situation.
> *"If you hadn't done that, I wouldn't be in this position."* Or *"Did you know this was happening?"*
- They wait for your guilt to kick in so you will bail them out.

Panic or Impulsiveness: They are *frenzied.* (They cry, jump around the room, can't sit down, converse irrationally and demonstrate illogical thought processes.) They keep say-

ing the same thing over and over again as if they want to make sure you've heard them.
- They wait to hear you say, "Calm down. *We* can solve this problem. It's not as bad as it seems. I know what we can do."

Dependence: They *play* to your sense of honor.
> *"You're good at doing this. Can you fix it?"* Or *"I'm not like you and I don't have the experience or the guts to do this. I don't think I can."*

- They want you to throw on your silk cape and say, "Have no fear, I'll save you," and own their problem.

Control: They *maintain constant control* of the situation. (They issue orders, and eliminate any opportunities for mutual resolution.)
> "You *have to do this*" Or "You *got us here*, you *fix it.*" Or "You *know what caused it*, you *fix it.*" Or "What are you *going to do about it?*"

- They wait and badger until you assume the problem without any resistance.

Denial: They *deny* the issue.
> *"Hey, no problem. What's the big deal?"*

- They hope you will pick up the debris and run with it. They want to hear you say, "Well, it's important to me and I think we need to do it." Or "Don't sweat it."

Aggression and Anger: They give physical and verbal *expressions* of frustration, fear, or threats.
> *"How could this happen? I'm not letting them get away with this. I want revenge."*

- They hope their out-of-control state will be cured. They want to hear you say, "Calm down. I can fix this and make the problem go away so we don't have to deal with it." They know you can get rid of this one for them.

Whatever behavior you observe, you are being put in the position to potentially be hooked into owning the problem. If you would like a method to keep people owning their own problem, refer to the list of skills given in the "Their Problem" oval in the diagram on page 24.

When it is "Their Problem," remember that whatever skill you choose to use, other people have the choice to accept or reject your style. When going through your skill options, you can:

- **listen**—in this way you acknowledge that you have heard what they have said

- **rephrase what you hear**—use more neutral language to refocus the discussion

- **probe**—asking open-ended questions to seek more information allowing people to view the situation from another perspective

- **validate**—identify and state the emotions they are feeling toward this situation—this lets them know that you understand what is important to them

- **brainstorm**—help create options for possible solutions to the problem (not options for you to solve it, but options that *they* can use to solve it)

- **coach**—ask the right questions and feed back the information to people in such a way that they are able to create for themselves a new direction and plan

- **clarify values and issues**—help them determine and identify what's important to them

- **defuse anger and frustration**—this allows people to feel they've been heard

The set of the skills listed in the "Their Problem" oval can be used to help people understand that it is *their* problem and you as the naked manager can help them decide what direction *they* will take next to resolve the problem. Using these skills will help them understand consequences and allow *them* to examine if they can live with those consequences.

My Problem

The next part of the equation is dealing with issues that are "My Problem." I use the term "equation" because the skill sets used for "My Problem" are added to the ones used *in* "Their Problem." The combination of this set of skills is used in solving your own problems.

As a manager, it is important that you accept responsibility for your own actions. The situation is "my problem" when one or more of the following characteristics are present:

- you find the behavior unacceptable

- someone's actions interfere with yours

- your needs are not met

The skill options or approaches to use for "My Problem" include:

- **manage conflict**—assess how you got to this point and what your needs and wants are for resolution. This is then followed by an action plan.

- **make a decision**—choose a course of action and act on it. Things don't get done if they stay in the idea stage

- **take risks**—have the courage to take action on what you believe. "If you always do what you've always done, then you'll always get what you've always got."

- **be flexible**—be open to listening and accepting possible solutions

- **confront**—address and negotiate the issue rather than avoid it

- **gather information**—use your support network to obtain different perspectives on and solutions to the issue

- **create an action plan**—establish a course of action to achieve results

Our Problem

When two people decide to mutually own a problem, the first step is to acknowledge that both parties are in this together and it is a joint decision.

Then, *and only then*, with acknowledgment does it become "Our Problem." When you define an issue as "Our Problem" you combine all the strategies and approaches in each of the ovals ("Their Problem" and "My Problem" and "Our Problem").

The additional skill options used for "Our Problem" include:

- **involve each party**—make sure everyone feels invested in the solution

- **enlist commitment**—identify people's needs and wants and attempt to address them; this will also yield better follow-through on actions

- **delegate**—appreciate different styles for accomplishment and let everyone own a piece of the problem

- **collaborate**—brainstorm many ideas to potentially meet everyone's interests

- **understand roles**—help determine expectations, tasks, and purposes

- **encourage**—keep up momentum for action through rewards, recognition, and appreciation

- **facilitate**—ensure everyone feels heard and each issue is addressed

- **trust**—build individual confidence and eliminate fear as an operating principle

One of the most important actions that the problem solving naked manager takes is to *not* take on someone else's problems without acknowledgment from both parties.

Rx for Problems

Problem solving, like postoperative treatment calls for different strategies. If you reflect on the entire model, you will notice that the skills used for "Their Problem" are the ones commonly used by managers, coaches, and counselors. The skills used for "My Problem" are effective in solving your own issues. And the skills used in "Our Problem" are ones used in partnerships, organizations, teams, and marriages.

This problem ownership model helps you decide which technique to take when other people's needs are not met. Now that you know you have a choice, ask yourself which specific approach you will choose the next time someone comes to you and says, "Toni didn't get the report written, and now I can't do my piece."

- "Is this *my* problem?" And "Will I take ownership of it?"

- "Is it *their* problem? And "Do I want to solve it for them?"

- " Is it *our* problem?" And "How can I keep all the issues separate until we acknowledge this is our problem?"

Prescribing the proper treatment for a problem will keep you and your organization healthy. Healing and survival depend on keeping all vital organs working.

Problem-solving ownership is about keeping your priorities and perspective in order.

Solutions from the collective wisdom

- Learn from experience, and don't be afraid to try new behaviors.
- Think of ways that everyone can win and benefit from the solutions.
- Remember to laugh when things get tough—a sense of humor is critical.
- Separate yourself from the situation—depersonalize it and approach it from another angle.
- Be open to other people's issues, but don't automatically assume they are *your* issues.
- Leave problems at the office—they can ruin your personal life.
- Facilitate and negotiate discussions.
- Accept that what can't be done today can be done tomorrow.
- Think before you speak, and don't get into situations that you are not prepared for.
- Recognize what you are capable of doing and do your best at it.
- Don't think that you have to do and solve it all.
- Believe in yourself and others—give them a chance to become great.

4

Exposing Yourself
Being Au Naturel from All Angles

When I was little, one of my favorite television shows was "Bewitched." The character Samantha, played by Elizabeth Montgomery, was a "good" witch. She was deeply in love with and married to a mortal man, Darrin. She wanted to experience life as a 60s suburban housewife. Samantha's mother, Endora, also a witch, was not impressed with mortal life and spent many of the sitcom episodes casting spells to prove a point or add some element of humor to her day. Samantha successfully dealt with the many witchcraft problems presented to her and, by the end of every half-hour time slot, she had produced a happy ending.

One "Bewitched" episode etched a lasting memory in my mind. Endora cast a spell on all the mortals so that they could only respond with complete honesty. They said exactly how they felt and truthfully stated their impressions. Chaos reigned. Relationships crumbled and people sought revenge for the audacity of someone making such truthful comments to them. What struck me was the similarity between this sitcom situation and reality. As a society, we place high regard for truth and honesty in our relationships. In reality, it is very difficult for human beings, mortals, to give and accept the truth.

The honesty I am referring to, and endorsing, is the truth of your convictions, your beliefs, and your passions about issues. It is the truth about who you are. The key to being able to expose your beliefs authentically is to know the techniques and to understand the listener with whom you are dealing. Often communications like these are difficult because all people receive information in different ways and from different frames of reference.

Exposing your beliefs and viewpoints is critical in developing good personal relationships. Revealing these beliefs and viewpoints in a truthful and honest way that people can hear is an art form, and one necessary to master for creating successful encounters. A naked manager has removed the many layers of protection and "fence-sitting" skills acquired over years of business dealings. Naked managers expose their core values and inner thinking in a way that lets others know what they stand for, believe in, and give credence to. If you choose not to expose yourself, people won't know your passions. If people don't know your passions, they may believe you lack opinion, substance, or soul. Opening yourself up, sharing your purity of conviction, is the first step to unlocking the doors that keep relationships closed.

Risking the Elements

Exposure has two key elements. The first is knowing *what* to expose—your truths, passions, and convictions. The second is understanding *how* to expose yourself when dealing with different personalities and ranks.

It is risky business to expose yourself and go "au naturel". Yet in today's intense business climate, exposure and visibility are crucial for all managers to gain and practice. If your colleagues don't have an understanding of your fundamental principles or what you are capable of doing, your career as a manager will be a lonely uphill battle.

One manager I spoke with said, "If you don't get out there and talk with people, you will die on the corporate vine. People will easily forget you if you don't get face-to-face time with them. In this world you won't go anywhere unless people think you are doing something and represent something."

A manager must be visible. Sitting safely in a cozy corner office may be comfortable, but it won't let people know the source and intensity of your passions and values—nor will it enhance your career. When you expose yourself, you acquire a public reputation. Whether good or bad, your opening up *will* have an effect.

Some individuals will listen to your perspective with the "thanks, but I'm out of here" response. They don't want to know and they don't want to get involved. Others will appreciate your stance or opinion. When you self-disclose, you increase trust in the relationship. You create a standard for honesty and a new code of ethics. Truth promotes trust.

As a young nun Mother Theresa was almost forced to leave two religious communities she worked in because of her vision of service to the poor. This passion was more intense than the other sisters could abide. Mother Theresa didn't sit around quietly with a few people and discuss what she believed and what she wanted changed. She acted and exposed herself to both sides of the warring parties. Similarly, naked managers talk openly and demonstrate what they passionately believe in and represent, to all levels involved.

Exposure and visibility is three-directional: up, down and sideways. You expose yourself personally and visually to your superiors, your peers, and your subordinates. The purpose and desired perception for each direction varies, but the goal is the same: *expose your convictions for the benefit of effecting results within the relationship.* This is the key to going au naturel as a "naked manager".

Some managers fear exposing their personal traits and the intensity of their beliefs. Their self-protection comes from the fear that the exposure will result in loss of position or power. They believe that if they tell too much, others will have ammunition or information to use against them. If they tell others about themselves, they create a more equal, reciprocal relationship, one that closes the distance between ranks.

Other managers are closet exhibitionists. They are confident in their convictions when they are alone or talking to someone who does not have a vested interest in the issue, but they hide their beliefs in public. This fear activates them to a style of distance management—"let's keep our distance. If you get too close to the real me, I'll feel too vulnerable." This sense of vulnerability might come from a fear of appearing inadequate, a lack of confidence in one's ability, a belief that one's opinion will not be valued, or a concern that expressing oneself will result in getting fired. Responding to these fears , distance managers "clothe" themselves for protection and make their relationships more aloof. The individuals they manage begin to create boundaries and walls to help them blend into the company's scenery and norms. Ashleigh Brilliant says, "If we all conceal our embarrassing peculiarities, we'll never know how many of us have them."[2] If people never show their "parts" how can we know what's natural and common? How can people know how they fit into their environment?

Some managers choose to never expose their personal beliefs for fear of standing out in the crowd. Ironically, those unique traits or actions might possibly be the very traits that make them valuable as employees. Yet no one will know their opinions and gifts because they have hidden and protected them from people. When I spoke with one wise naked manager, he gave this advice:

> "If you are comfortable in your home, comfortable in your management job, you are doing something wrong. If you are too comfortable, then business competition will whip you. You have to think in the future, act in the present, and expose yourself to what's out there."

Exposure and its resulting interactions add meaning and purpose to actions. And actions can have wide-reaching effects. I would rather have a manager who represents and stands for something than one that has no opinion or spine at all. Personally I am not known for following a person who is morally bankrupt or lacks opinion. I want to know what a person is made of. How about you? Exposing and communicating your convictions and beliefs is key to establishing yourself as a successful manager.

Anyone who flies an airplane knows that when taking off, you must fly *into* the wind. If a pilot would stop to fear the strong pressure, the plane might crash. When managers push forward beyond established boundaries and maneuver through the force of the wind of self-initiating, they are willing to soar. Those who can't expose themselves stay on the ground unrecognized, unseen, and forgotten. They may also be perceived as not having any beliefs or convictions. To have an opinion and voice is a great way to get off the ground.

Exposure (upwards, downwards, sideways and in all directions)

You cannot expose yourself only to specific levels in an organization. Exposure requires balance in all directions.

If you expose yourself . . .

> *only up*, it is career suicide; you will be thought of as only out for yourself

only down, you get a very limited view; it is difficult for
inspiration and change

only sideways, you become one of the many, and can
lose your individuality

in all directions, you maintain balance and achieve results

Exposing Upwards

There is a time to be clothed and a time to be naked. It is
an unfortunate reality that, with upward exposure, we wear
more masks and clothes. We cover ourselves and are less
likely to be open because our vulnerability is greater. You
feel you are being observed under a microscope.

Watch out for the people who focus their visibility only
upwards. They may be thought of as great people and are fre-
quently promoted, but they tend to be glory-seeking, taking
credit for others' accomplishments. They are often ambi-
tious, untrustworthy, and, in the long run, ineffective. They
don't always view the big picture—only the one that makes
them look like the winner.

Many managers panic at the idea of openly exposing
themselves upwards to their supervisors. Yet on reflective
analysis they discover that the most significant times in their
careers occurred when they established open rapport. Their
openness built trust, respect, and a career path.

Exposing Sideways

It is easy to exposure yourself only to your peers. You can
swap stories, build alliances, and complain about why things
don't get done. Your colleagues understand and can relate to
what is going on. Investing your energy solely in this direction can cause you to be viewed as part of the club, one of the
"good ole boys", one of *them!*

Building a network and support system is valuable in
any career. The concept of two heads are better than one has
been valuable for many years. Having a peer group made up
of individuals who can approach an issue from different

perspectives and exposures can be energizing, influential, and dynamic.

Managers need to be cautious about people who focus their visibility only sideways. They want to be recognized and associated with a particular group. They may put aside their own opinions and gain strength from a common consensus. Their source of power may come from position and perception, not from good work and potential.

Exposing Downwards

Here is the area where you have the power advantage. People are more likely to believe you because of your knowledge and position. Exposing your beliefs can charge your employees and boost your confidence.

Watch out for the people who focus their visibility only downwards. They may fear making waves in upwards or sideways directions and may not have developed effective strategies or the right connections to get things done. Their motives may come from a desire to control rather than contribute. Often for these people, their talk is big but their results are small.

Exposure Importance

Formulating a sense of partnership and responsibility for accomplishments creates commitment and performance from individuals who have placed trust in their supervisor. For this reason exposing yourself in all directions is important to continually do.

Bad Optics

If you are ever perceived as focusing in any direction (up, down, or sideways) for the sole purpose of working the optics you've blown it. Portraying the "image" rather than "conviction" will in the long run demonstrate that you stand for nothing. If you are perceived as a fake, your days are short-lived. If your are perceived as having a soul and a belief, your value increases.

A simple explanation of this concept can be seen in the following chart:

Direction of Exposure / Behaviors for Exposure	Perceptions *Expressed and Desired*		Purpose *Intention and Goal*	
Exposure to Superiors	• stable • able • qualified • committed • organized	• passionate • enthusiastic • nonantagonistic • well-prepared *(action = words)*	*to:* • understand purpose • understand facts • understand system • enhance network • implement agendas	• impact actions • be recognized • be mentored • influence decisions
Exposure to Peers	• candid • direct • compatible • equal	• one of the team • partner • collaborator • comradery	*to:* • build alliances • have a sounding board	• gain support • build connections
Exposure to Subordinates	• leader • fair • fearless • accessible	• one of us • not a doormat • informed • knowledgeable	*to:* • create teamwork • gain commitment	• build trust • gain support
Exposure to All	• leader • respected • responsible • credible • reliable • honest • invested • capable • competent • composed	• dependable • has conviction • fair • trustworthy • knowledgeable • professional • has common sense • positive • emotionally controlled	*to:* • network • demonstrate consistency • sell yourself • gain interdependence • gather information • provide answers to questions • foster clear communication • build partnerships • enable information sharing • understand other perspectives • establish direct line connections • create mutual understanding on critical issues	

Exposing through approach

Psychologist Carl Jung took the approach . . . don't listen to the words, watch what the feet do.[3] By watching the actions and behavioral patterns of an individual, you can *truly* determine what an individual represents and what is important to him or her. Those who say they will do something and consistently fail to act are exposing their true opinion on the subject. It is not what a person says but what a person does that speaks the truth of his or her conviction.

Consistency displays conviction. It is appropriate and essential in all levels of exposure. As a rule of thumb, use the Zen approach for exposure—consider the whole, not just a part. Expose yourself in a way that allows people to understand you are acting in the best interest of the *entire* company, not just one department or one group. This is the best way to "win" all around.

Exposing through emotions

Why does it seem so odd and uncomfortable to expose our true emotions? State laws govern the physical aspect of exposure, and somehow we have outlawed the exposure of our true self as well. We often get stuck on how to really speak clearly about our emotions. Soul, sensitivity, excitement, spirit, seat of passion, being, and opinion are emotional words that tell of a deeper part of self and support courageous behavior that leads to independence, achievement, and choice. Perhaps expressing an emotion is difficult because there is a little voice in our head that says, "You shouldn't feel that; it's bad." Many times people choose to keep closed and detached. Yet emotions are natural and indicate inner responses. Real leadership is a gut-level action and requires a display of controlled emotions.

Managers who display passion make people want to join them. Sharing an emotion can move the group process forward more quickly and increase the organization's level of performance.

The most moving presentation of conviction is personal, almost emotional. One of the most powerful political speeches was given by Republican Bob Dole when he announced his resignation from the Senate to run for president in 1996. He cried. It moved people because they saw the person inside, the *real* person. They identified with Bob Dole's humanity. Exposure of feelings and beliefs is best done in a positive way. If your exposure of emotions is constantly negative and deals with disappointments, a sense of being overwhelmed, or annoyance with people, you will lose your followers. Emotional exposure quite often expresses passionate, internal commitment and deeply rooted thoughts. Communicating your emotions helps get people to follow you, embrace your vision, and join your team.

When you demonstrate emotion you demonstrate that there is more to you than what's on the surface. You show people you have a soul, a belief, a conviction, and an approach. It's hard to lie when you are exposed. People will learn quickly that what they see is what they get. This exposure can build a sense of trust in the people around you. Openly confronting issues and expressing your beliefs helps the whole organizational environment build honesty and trust.

Conclusion

If you have difficulty discovering your own strong passions for life, ask yourself if there is something you continuously defend. Chances are there is a deep belief behind your defense. Robert Muller, former assistant secretary general of the United Nations, passionately said,

> "You are a free immensely powerful source of life and goodness. Affirm it. Spread it. Radiate it. Think day and night about it. And you will see a miracle happen in the greatness of your own life."

Driving in England one year, my concentration was on motorways, roundabouts, and driving on what I thought was the "wrong" side of the road. All the newness had me staying alert. In one small English town I came upon a road sign, which read "Change Priorities Ahead." I thought I had just entered the twilight zone or maybe a scene out of *LA Story*, where road signs communicate life directions for Steve Martin's destiny. Change my priorities? Here? In England? In fact the sign meant the direction of traffic was changing. For me, it meant I should take a look at how I was functioning and how effective my actions were—as it should for you!

As a naked manager, have the courage to change your priorities and expose yourself from all angles (from verbalizing what you enjoy, to having the courage to admit your mistakes). If people criticize you, they are only showing their ignorance. They are demonstrating that they don't have a depth of understanding or a realization about the importance of having passion, soul, conviction, or belief. It is these components that add to one's credibility. The more you reveal or expose about yourself, the more you can appreciate, value, and create effective work relationships—in all directions. Your network can help make things happen for you, but first you must expose yourself to that network. It is your consistent optimism and uncomplicated straightforwardness that will demonstrate that you are comfortable with your nakedness and with who you are.

Take the risk and expose yourself.

"To laugh is to risk appearing the fool,
   To weep is to risk appearing sentimental,
   To reach out to others is to risk getting involved,
   To show your feelings is to risk exposing yourself,
   To place your ideas and dreams before the crown is to
      risk their loss,
   To love is to risk not being loved in return,
   To hope is to risk pain,
   To try is to risk failure,
   But risk must be taken because the greatest hazard in
      life is to risk nothing,
   People who risk nothing, do nothing, have nothing,
   They may avoid suffering and sorrow, but they simply
      cannot learn, feel, change, grow, live or love,
   Chained by their certitudes, they are a slave,
   Only the person who risks is free."

Anonymous

EXPOSURE EXERCISE

The principle of exposure proposes that in order to lead and manage people you must first have depth and conviction. You must understand what is important to you, what you are passionate about, and what you value. In this understanding lies the foundation for all meaningful actions. Before you can expose yourself it is essential to determine what you *have* to

Decide on what you value	**What do I passionately believe in?**
	Why?
	And why is that?
	And why is that?
	the answer to this final "why" question will more closely reveal what you are really passionate about
Be decisive	**What can I do to expose myself more?**
	How?
	When?
	Why?
What are the barriers?	**What is preventing me from exposing myself?**
	What?
	What else?
	What else?
Action	**What is the first action step I need to take to become successful?**
	When?
	What is my reward?
	What will motivate me?

expose and what you *want* to expose. Our soft spots are often our blind spots. By answering the exposure exercise questions, you can increase your personal awareness and get closer to your true self, your soul.

Solutions from the collective wisdom

- Keep your mind and attitudes positive.

- Know that deep down you have the strength to do things.

- Keep your résumé updated—it helps remind you of your skills.

- Don't be afraid to let others learn more than you do—it can only improve their performance.

- Concentrate on doing the best you can with the present opportunity.

- Don't sweat the small stuff.

- Be frank in your approach.

- Keep problems in perspective—business is not life or death.

- Keep your priorities straight; ask yourself, "Will babies die if this decision is not made?"

- Expect a lot from yourself, and be content with your growth.

- Don't ask anyone to do something you wouldn't do yourself.

- Have enthusiasm and persistence.

- Evaluate where you have been and how you got there—learn from it.

5

Big Buts

Positive Attitudes and Creative Minds

The entertainer Pee Wee Herman once said, "The trouble with the world is that everyone's got a big but." My advice to managers is to take your *but* and put it somewhere else.

"But" is a fascinating word. It has the ability to erase everything that has preceded it For example, if a manager says, "Toni, you are a great worker. And perfect for this job. It is always a comfort to know we can depend on you, *but* there is one thing I want to tell you." When Toni hears that "but," everything initially said becomes secondary or forgotten. A sense of caution occurs within the person, suggesting the real issue is about to be spoken.

That big old "but" can squash things flat and leave a nasty odor once it's gone. "Buts" stifle creativity and motivation, creating a good news-bad news style that leaves the listener feeling mistrusting or apprehensive. Encouraging creativity and innovation within yourself and your organization helps; maintain the competitive edge, increase productivity, and add enjoyment to work. For a manager, this concept of keeping a positive attitude and fostering creativity is crucial in today's business environment.

While giving a workshop on creativity I was brainstorming with a group of managers to create a "but" substitute. When one manager offered the word "however" as an alternative, another woman in the group spoke up and said, "'However' is simply a 'classy but'!" She was right; using the word "however" doesn't change the impact of the message, it merely softens the blow.

My advice to that group of managers and to you is to replace the word "but" with the word "and." Miraculously, this word makes a wonderful transition to the next topic and keeps the interaction going in an upward, innovative motion. For example: "Chris, I can tell you like your job here at XYZ *and* one of the things I want to point out about the work you're doing is . . . ." Substituting the word "and" makes for an amazing change. Pee Wee was right: big "buts" drag you down, stifling your creativity, and the urge to try. In the business climate of today the people who move forward are those who are innovative and don't limit themselves by:

- "but we can't"
- 'but what about"
- "but we've tried it before"
- "but it costs too much"
- "but I'm tired"
- "but I can't"

So take your big "but" and put it somewhere else.

Reducing the size of your "but"

Think of your circle of contacts. You will probably recognize that some individuals are more creative than others. Why? Some attribute their creative gift to their upbringing; for many individuals their innovative spirit has been mothered by necessity. Others say they eat the right foods or that they are destined to be creative. I've even heard some attribute the reason for their creativity to a very creative astrological chart.

We all have the ability to be creative (*all* of us, even you!). There is no excuse for not being creative. As a colleague of mine says, "If you have ever cooked with hamburger meat, you are creative!" While studying a group of individuals, researchers found that creative people thought they were creative whereas less creative people thought they were not creative. It is all a matter of giving yourself creative license to use the talents you already possess. Often all it takes to reduce the size of your "but" is to see situations as possibilities rather than anchors. If you sit around moping and criticizing all day, your "but" will only get bigger. The longer a person believes in something, the more unquestioned and inflexible he or she becomes. If this is your mode of operation, it may be time to give yourself a good swift kick in the "but" and begin to imagine new possibilities and alternatives.

When people initially come up with ideas or answers, it is often without thought, in response to an internal emotion. Their reaction is from a personal perspective or need. Pausing for a moment before responding with an answer allows a brief moment to think, assess the situation, and consider different perspectives. This might be all it takes to change a negative "but" thought into a creative opportunity with positive possibilities and alternatives. Naked managers who skillfully direct a perception in a more positive vein can more easily motivate both others and themselves. Being a positive leader helps increase and maximize the performance of people.

The following are some examples for turning negative thoughts into positive ones:

Negative:
"It's nice out, but there's a 30% chance of rain."
Positive:
"It's nice out and there's a 70% chance of sun."

Negative:
"I work here, but this job stinks."
Positive:
"I work here and I realize that
things need to change."

Negative:
"You might think it's funny, but this is the
worse thing that could happen."
Positive:
"You might think it's funny and you now have possibly
the best learning experience of a lifetime."

Taking time to think of issues from a different perspective can quickly reduce the size of your "but" by relaxing the negative rigidity of your mind-set. Creating, visioning, dreaming, call it what you want, the first step happens in the mind. Fostering a positive attitude not only affects your work; it greatly affects those around you.

We all have a rack of "bad tapes" in our unconscious mind. These are the little voices playing in our heads that come from past experiences, values handed down to us in our childhood, and pointed fingers with big SHOULD signs attached to them ("you should do this, you should do that"). I say, stop "shoulding" yourself. Allow yourself to have fun, make hard choices, stand up for yourself, take risks, and be you. Remember, even when you are falling on your face, you are moving forward!

Prescription for Reducing Your Big But
and opening your creative mind

Here are four key elements to use when you pursue "but" reduction:

1. Items are not always intended to be used for their specific purpose.

2. *Every* event is an opportunity.

3. The sphere of options is vast and often unrelated.

4. "What if" and "Why not" open the steel trapdoors to the creative mind.

I cannot emphasize enough the importance of humor and fun in this creative process. These are tools that can transport you to different mind-sets. They can help dig you out of a rut and get you onto a different thought train. When I conduct creativity workshops I sometimes bring in crayons to smell and draw with. They jog the senses and bring back old memories. (Playing old songs also works well.) I will blow bubbles and hand out lollipops. It is hard to be negative with a lollipop in your mouth and bubbles floating around the room (even a boardroom!). These are all precipitators for thinking differently, getting unstuck, and imagining the endless possibilities. It is almost like getting back to a childlike time, free from inhibitions. I encourage you to play, be silly, and open your mind to possibilities.

When I worked in an insurance company, I quickly realized I would soon shrivel up from boredom and repetition. To spice things up I decided to create a happy minute. I was tired of watching this huge room of deadpan faces sitting at their desks putting in time. At precisely 3:00 p.m. every day I would sit in my office chair and spin around in circles for one minute. "*But* we shouldn't do that," the masses cried. "*But* we might get fired." The dull panicked. I pointed out that it was only a one-minute event and I felt much better afterward. Within a week, more people had joined my cause and life was enjoyable in the insurance company if only for one minute. All of this has to do with opening up your mind and thinking differently.

Here are some challenging questions for you. What else could you use a fork for? Think of the possibilities. Campbell's Soup stretched the limits and created the concept of "Chunky Soup." How about beginning a meeting with it? How about including it with your next correspondence? The possibilities are endless and encouraged. What else could your organization use to enhance its performance? Naked managers imagine and create. This helps make work enjoyable and revitalizes people.

Take a creative, fun break
Don't give up too easily, stretch your mind and imagine the possibilities you can create—and remember, no buts!

Create pictures with the fragments below.

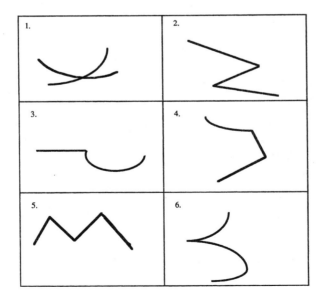

Buts and no buts

It is my belief that in an organization people fall into four zones: Batteries, Dynamics, Statics, and Chargers (see diagram below). Recognizing and encouraging capacity and generation within the organization creates an environment where "buts" are taken as challenges to make things happen. Not attending to these areas can short circuit the system and important energy can be lost.

Organizational Action Model

"Batteries" (stored voltage)	"Dynamics" (energetic and powerful)
"Statics" (force at rest)	"Chargers" (ready for action)

↑ Capacity

Generation →

The capacity axis refers to the ability, talent, qualification, power and competencies a person possesses. The generation axis refers to the ability a person possesses to produce, originate, put into motion, formulate and invent concepts and results.

I define each of these zones in the following ways.

The Statics are happy just where they are. They seek stability. They are comfortable with their situation, and don't want anything to change for fear of upsetting the status quo. Their experience and education has brought them this far, and that is all they believe they need. "Nothing new or different please, I'll do just what I'm told," is their petition. Their source of energy for being creative is in a resting state.

The Batteries can be counted on to do the job well. They have the capacity to accomplish the task as requested. They have a knowledge of what is right and true. They do what is expected of them—no more and no less. "I know how to do this job as it is, please don't ask me to change, I don't want to use up my energy," is their petition. They are quick to tell you, "but we have never done it that way before, this tried and true way is right." Their creative minds will work only within the confines of the job and the space. They protect their voltage.

The Chargers are sometimes perceived as bulls in a china shop. They need reining in. They are filled with a wealth of new and bright ideas, yet lack the experience and expertise to master the job at hand. They have free spirited desires to do, try, and experiment. They are ready to be molded into the organization's culture. "Give me a chance, I want to try" is their petition. There is no "but" that can stop them. Their creative minds are fresh and without war wounds. They can invigorate an organization.

The Dynamics are ready for action. They are skilled, pumped, equipped, and charged to meet the challenges that face them. They challenge the status quo. "Let me do it, I know how and I can envision a great change" is their petition. They have a high positive attitude and level of confidence. They think creatively and can quickly come up with solutions for the issues that face them. Their minds are open, and experience has filled them with confidence. They wisely understand the perspectives of others. Their actions come from the head, not the ego. Dynamics are willing to increase learning.

The proportion of workers falling into the Dynamic category is low yet desired in today's workforce. The new workforce rules say if you are not challenging the status quo you are not doing what you are supposed to do as a manager and leader. Both the Chargers and the Dynamics are likely to be viewed by the organization as people with potential, who have put their "big but" aside to accomplish all there is to accomplish.

The Making of a Dynamic Employee

Dynamics are curious.

The urge to try, is strongly linked to curiosity, and innovation. "Business has only two basic functions—marketing and innovation," according to Peter Drucker.[4] Curious people wonder what tornadoes sounded like before steam trains were invented! Being innovative means having the willingness and desire to explore, attempt and achieve. It is making the quantum leap from "what has always been done" to "how can we do it better." Innovative, naked managers are willing to open their minds and consider the situation from different angles.

Dynamics are creative.

Generation is an important component of creativity. A person must twist, divide, elaborate, conjure up, and develop thoughts to produce a creative idea. Creative thinkers combine capacity and generation to take initiative instead of waiting to be told what to do. They generate useful alternatives and make decisions. Dynamics solve problems and design ways to move forward. When confronted with issues, they take risks and have an open mind to the expanded number of possibilities for a solution. Naked managers are sensitive to and value the abilities of a creative mind. They know that the mind is a powerful tool that can greatly affect actions.

Dynamics are not swayed by the routine.

I am astonished at how easy it is to program our minds and alter our thoughts or actions. Let me give you a quick example.

Spell the word "spot" out loud. What do you do when you come to a green light? If you said "stop," you, like most people, had the subliminal message change your way of thinking. If you said "go," congratulations! Not only do you have basic road sense; you also were not easily swayed by the hidden message. Try this quick exercise on friends and co-workers. You will be astounded at how many people give the "stop" answer. Why? The answer is simple: it is easy to program our way of thinking, thus creating habits, standards, norms, and routines.

If it is this easy to alter thinking and program thoughts, imagine what other messages your mind is dealing with. What other deviations have effects on your thought process that limit you from becoming a Dynamic? The unconscious mind is a powerful driving force for all humans. Your interactions as a manager have the ability to program the thinking of others towards more positive and innovative approaches to situations. As demonstrated above, it can be as easy as using the right kinds of words to revitalize and motivate you and your staff toward the Dynamic category and away from being guided by convention.

Questions for challenging routines

- What makes this so hard? What can you do right now to change it?

- Why does this always get done this way? How can we do it better?

- Did it work yesterday or the day before? Today, let's do something different.

- I'm going to run this meeting backwards and see if we can improve the results.

- Today, I'll do your job and you do mine. Let's compare notes tomorrow.

- Let's imagine we're on vacation and this is what we do for enjoyment.

Dynamics have an attitude.

Of all the bare essentials for a naked manager, personal attitude is the most important. Your attitude is paramount to your effectiveness. In several reports, when companies and employees were evaluated on why they were successful, the same answer continued to surface: *attitude*. Naked managers who feel helpless and hopeless and believe the world and their organization have done them wrong are prime candidates for spiraling down into the pit of doom and gloom. Those who believe they are stripped of integrity, ingenuity, and individualism follow career paths that no longer hold promise and hope. Their sense of worthlessness moves them away from being C.E.D.'s (Chief Executive Dynamos)! Belief and desire make things happen. Your attitude affects your destiny. I'm not saying we should all misbehave, simply acquire an attitude that looks as though you could! Fostering an open mind set with a slant on enjoyment makes life an exciting opportunity.

Naked managers can develop and encourage creative and innovative mind-sets and attitudes by valuing broad-based thinking that:

- makes things happen

- develops new processes

- implements plans

- brings about change

Naked managers are not burdened with shoulds, procedures, and buts, for these only stifle the generating and developing of new ideas. Change is part of our life; it is constant. Trying to keep things the same keeps capacity and generation low and definitely short circuits the organization and the employee. If you "always do what you've always done, then you always get what you always got." Open your mind and the minds of others with comments like "what if," "how about," or "maybe we could." These get individuals motivated to find solutions to challenges . For naked managers, a competency for success is boldness. "There is no honor is just doing the job." One manager once told me, "Honor comes from a willingness to do something new and bold and with the highest standard possible." Success comes from being dynamic.

Naked managers get rid of negative wardrobes and put on positive attires that don't emphasize their "big but"!

Solutions from the collective wisdom

- Stop dwelling on past issues and how you feel wronged; take charge of you career and future, and make things happen.
- Always try to improve the way you do things.
- Practice being creative.
- Make time to understand your employees and their respective work.
- Read inspiring material and apply it to your life.
- Pursue ideas and thoughts from reading and talking to others.
- Try to look at the big picture, and don't get bogged down by the little things.
- Create alternatives to different situations; don't be stuck with only one solution.
- Expand on existing ideas.
- Spend time with people who spark your imagination.
- Keep a desire to be successful.
- Don't believe you can't do it.
- Give yourself permission to do what you dream.
- Find people with like minds to support your ideas.
- Realize you can't please everybody, but you can make it better.
- Don't compromise your standards because people are not enthusiastic or are lazy.

6

Birthmarks
Using Uniqueness to Your Advantage

During a family discussion one evening, my son asked my husband why he was attracted to me. I held my breath, not sure if I could deal with the response. "I liked your mom from the very beginning because she wasn't like other women; she was different," my husband explained (points for my husband). "She's not different, Dad, she's crazy!" my son exclaimed (no points for my son!).

Thankfully, we are all distinctly different from every other person on earth. Your differences abound, both mentally and physically. Medical doctors tell us that each body reacts differently to injury, stress, and treatment, *depending on the person*. Similarly psychometric instruments demonstrate that we have different personality preferences and styles. When I administer personality assessments, my clients usually have one of four comments:

1. "Now I understand why I am doing these things."

2. "Now I understand why that other person is doing these things."

3. "All this time I thought I was stupid or weird. Now I understand this is the way I do it and it's okay."

4. "I know. I just wish other people realized it."

What these individuals are discovering is that they are different and unique. My son may define these differences as "crazy." But nonetheless I value my differences, my free spirit, my uniqueness. I realize it is my strength for forming relationships and accomplishing tasks. These distinguishing features are my personality birthmarks.

Birthmark characteristics can be related to management:

1. A birthmark is a congenital mark on the skin of human beings that appears at birth or in later life and occasionally disappears spontaneously.
   ° Managers may have acquired their markings at birth or as they go through corporate life.

2. Birthmarks deepen in color when a person cries or exercises.
   ° Naked managers' distinguishing marks may become more evident and deepen with the intensity in the workplace. This managerial birthmark may be seen as a blotch or an unsightly imperfection by others in the organization.

3. Although sometimes best left untreated, treatment is dictated by the type of blemish.
   ° Managers can attempt to change or remove what they believe to be a disfiguring birthmark through training, coaching, or counseling.

4. Birthmarks affect all ethnic groups and are not gender-specific.
° Anyone can have a birthmark and a choice to value or devalue them.

Like birthmarks on the skin, managerial birthmarks can distinguish people as unique in their work environment and on the planet. When some people notice that someone is doing, saying, or thinking something different from their perspective, they can be challenged. Their fear about being different or having their beliefs endangered forces them to respond and protect themselves out of a need for sameness.

For some the issue of valuing differences does not hold the same benefits as the need for being alike. Yet the fact is, we are *not* all alike. To not value uniqueness is to not accept reality. If you don't accept who you are, who will you become?

Even the sun has spots! And some of them are hidden because when we look at the sun we only see half of it. The other side is hidden. If you want to understand the sun completely, you need to consider it in its entirety. If you want to understand people you need to recognize them in their entirety, from all sides, birthmarks and all. This is not an easy task. As humans we don't want to know too much about ourselves or others. Whether it is fear, lack of opportunity, or worrying, we tend to cover certain parts of ourselves as one might a birthmark.

In a 1989 survey of American habits, Portez and Sinrod found that 59% of those surveyed did not like the way they looked nude.[5] People do not like to look at the whole package. We hurry to hide our psychological birthmarks and neglect to recognize their potential power. When you remove the layers that hide your natural side, you begin to know who you really are. Simply put, when you get in the "buff" you get the bare facts!

I once had a job as an educator for the March of Dimes, a nonprofit organization that works with disabled individuals. I traveled with a physically disabled person to different schools educating children about disabilities and differences. The students' reactions to my partner varied. Some faces showed shock, bodies squirmed with discomfort, and others giggled for lack of knowing how to respond. Mostly, all the students were curious. They wanted to know, "What's wrong with you and what's it like to be that way?" By the end of each session, the students were armed with knowledge and became more comfortable with the disabled person and the concept of differences and uniqueness.

These students gave typical human responses. Searching for valuable talents, abilities, and uniqueness can be frightening. It is easy to list the negative traits of a person. (And if you are having any trouble assessing your negative traits, ask family members. They are sure to give you a laundry list of items!) There is no shortage of the negative input we can receive regarding our differences and unlikeability. When a level of awareness or comfort is raised about these issues, people can begin to perceive the negatives as having potentially positive possibilities.

America promotes the concept of freedom to be different and to make a difference. Team-building and human dynamic gurus will praise and promote the notion of valuing difference for a greater output. Practice denies the principle, for the majority of people have acquired an attitude (whether through the media, upbringing, values, or norms) that we "should" be like or better than other people, but certainly not different. People strive and strategize to make their bodies look like top models and to make their personalities resemble those of their idols. We compare ourselves to public figures, colleagues, and neighbors.

To combat this societal reality and avoid feelings of distress produced by comparison, we identify and join with people who are most like us. We find comfortable relationships with those who agree with us. When confronted with someone of an unlike mind, our feelings of frustration or inadequacy begin to emerge. We ask, "What's wrong with me?" Or wonder, "What's wrong with them?" Or question, "Why am I not like that?" We desperately want the ease that comes with being similar and deny the reality that we are all different—different with valuable talents.

I recently overheard a conversation while I was sitting in an old southern diner. A group of men had gathered around the table and were talking about a wide range of topics, from the best tobacco to chew to what the Republicans could do to better this country. The atmosphere was relaxed; no one was in a hurry to go anywhere. Everyone sat and drank their coffee and ate their grits.

One gentlemen, Dan, began to tell the story of his son's adventurous solo canoe trip down the Neuse River. He was obviously proud of his 18-year-old son's stamina and independence to attempt such a challenging endeavor. He told of the obstacles his son had to face. He related how the things he had taught his son could be used during the trip. Best of all, Dan told about the treasures his son had found. "My son dug into that river bank and found some fossils and bones. We took them to the university and found out that they dated back to the Paleozoic Era or even the Mesozoic Era." Dan beamed as he spoke about the treasures his son had discovered. He clearly was well informed on these prehistoric eras and wanted to share his wealth of knowledge and tell the group of his uniqueness.

I noticed not long into this fossil story that the gentlemen in the group began to lose total interest in what Dan had to say. Their eyes had that "deer in the headlight" look, as Dan regaled the story about his son and the fossils. Dan was obviously filled with pride and excitement about these treasures that now hung on the wall in his den. Yet it was easy to tell the group did not care about what Dan had to say—let alone get a history lesson in the diner. The gentlemen were merely waiting for the story to be over so they could move on to another topic. Dan sensed this, and you could see he was hurt because the group didn't find this information nearly as exciting as he did. I am sure he was experiencing a sense of annoyance for the lack of value these men seemed to place on something so obviously important and unique.

Dan's story ended and the group began discussing another political issue affecting farmland, farmers, and Republicans. At that point, a new member entered the diner, carrying a jar of figs. He told about how he had grown these figs and his wife had canned them. He described the figs in such a way that you could see the gentlemen's mouths watering as they listened to the description of these alluring figs.

"Well, open them up, Bob. Let's have some of them figs if they're so darn good."

Bob attempted to open the jar so he could pass them around and gloat about their great taste. Unfortunately, he was unable to open the jar. Several of the men attempted to break into the fig treasure, but no one was able to crack the seal. Want and desire was causing impatience in the group. Suddenly Dan offered his services. He was a well built man. He had put aside his annoyance with the group over the fossil story and grabbed for the fig jar. Without any effort Dan opened the jar and began passing it around. The group was thrilled and amazed. Instantly Dan was highly valued because of his ability. He became the hero, and the conversation continued for a long time about how great Dan was.

Understanding and appreciating our uniqueness and greatness is sometimes more difficult than accepting the fact that we don't have any. Individuals are often surprised at what qualities are of value to themselves and others. We all value different characteristics based on need. Don't underestimate your individual talents. *"You won't find in any park or city a monument to a committee."* Our society values individualism and the ability to be comfortable with oneself. Psychologist Maslow identifies reaching "optimal psychological adjustment" as a process, satisfying different need levels to reach the ultimate mind-set of "self-actualization." A naked manager strives to possess the 14 characteristics designated as necessary for being comfortable with self and one's abilities: (source: *An Introduction to Theories Of Personality*, Robert Ewen, 1980)

✔ **1. Accurate perception of reality:** free of unwarranted optimism, pessimism, and other defensive distortions of reality. Better able to distinguish between the real and phony and to judge things more accurately.

✔ **2. Greater acceptance of self and others:** more tolerant of human frailty and less judgmental of self and others. Less guilty about any personal shortcomings.

✔ **3. Greater spontaneity and self-knowledge:** more spontaneous and natural in behavior and better able to comprehend true motives, emotions, abilities, and potential. Guided by own code of ethics.

✔ **4. Devotion to excellence:** has a consuming mission in life that occupies much energy, often involving philosophical or ethical issues. Seeks to accomplish goals as well as is humanly possible.

✔ **5. Greater need for privacy and solitude:** healthy detachment due in part to the tendency to rely on own feelings and values, resulting in less need to ascertain the opinions of others.

✔ **6. Greater autonomy:** motivated by the need to fulfill own inner potentials rather than by the desire to seek external rewards or possessions. Demonstrates a relative independence of other people and the environment.

✔ **7. Greater appreciation:** lives a richer and more fulfilling life because cherishes the blessings already received and appreciates again and again the wonders of existence.

✔ **8. Greater frequency of peak experiences:** has mystical moments of absolute perfection and gets subsumed in feelings of ecstasy, wonder, and awe. These experiences may come from love, work, music, bursts of creativity, or moments of profound insight.

✔ **9. Greater social interest:** strongly identifies with the human species and has a genuine sympathy for and desire to help others.

✔ **10. Deeper, more loving interpersonal relationships:** prefers intimate and loving relationships with a few close friends, rather than superficial contacts with a wide variety of associates.

✔ **11. More democratic character structure:** has the ability to befriend people of all classes, races, and ethnic groups and often seems virtually unaware of such differences. Strongly opposed to injustice, inequality, cruelty, and the exploitation of others.

✔ **12. Greater discrimination between good and evil:** has strong moral and ethical standards and rarely vacillates as to course of action considered right or wrong. Typically accepts the responsibility for own actions rather than rationalizing or trying to blame errors on others.

✔ **13. More unusual sense of humor:** dislikes humor based on hostility or superiority such as ethnic or "insult" jokes. Prefers jokes that are more philosophical and instructive.

✔ **14. Greater creativity:** demonstrates a fresh and creative approach to life, developing unorthodox methods to problems.

"There are no perfect human beings," says Maslow.[6] Self-actualization is a matter of degree rather than an all-or-nothing affair. Moving toward being self-actualized is fundamental for the naked manager. It is one of the most important aspects of motivation, and is crucial to a person's effectiveness. This level of self-contentment does not stress navel gazing or looking only in the direction of self. It is about guiding your thoughts and actions toward becoming comfortable with your uniqueness, your abilities, and your birthmarks, as well as those of others. It is also closely linked to the qualities of the producer discussed in the previous chapter.

In Delphi, a town in ancient Greece, the words of the Greek philosopher Thales of Miletus from the year 600 B.C. are inscribed on the temple of Apollo. He writes, "Human greatness comes only from within. We must recognize our own strengths and limitations. By learning of our present condition we can structure a path for future behavior." Now almost 2,600 years later, that advice remains true. Your identity comes from within, not from without.

When you manage from this perspective you are willing to let go of the behaviors and thoughts that don't work for you anymore. People too often become limited by perception and sense of self. Naked managers are willing to take risks and explore limits. They recognize that mistakes are not sins, only ways of doing something different. Birthmarks are not bad; they are just the attributes of being unique. Naked managers perceive their birthmarks as springboards, not anchors. They recognize and avail themselves of their uniqueness. Remember, normal is a dryer setting, it is not something to strive for. You are a unique person with strengths, weaknesses and differences. To focus on your uniqueness and use it to your advantage is one way of achieving excellence and reaching your full potential. Linus the cartoon character from the Charlie Brown series says, "I can't live without that blanket, I can't face life unarmed." Each of us has great inner qualities. Use them rather than depending on some cloaking device.

The rules in business are changing. Employees must think of themselves as sole proprietors, responsible for their own career direction and success. You are in charge of promoting yourself (survival of the fittest seems to be becoming the employment norm), and your birthmarks can be your greatest strength and marketing tool. Without them you are a harmless void. Birthmarks are your unique signature.

Solutions from the collective wisdom

- Concentrate on your positive skills and transfer them to other attributes.

- Value your sense of humor—it is a wonderful gift.

- Think about how you treat people, what your actions are saying.

- Cherish your ability to encourage others to achieve their best.

- Don't be afraid to be you—that's who you are.

- Use your gifts and talents—they are your greatest resource.

- Have the courage to accept yourself; it's good when you are your own best friend.

- Do the best you can with your present opportunities and resources.

- Believe in yourself and the people you work with.

- Focus on your goals—it gives you a sense of direction.

7

From Ear to Ear
Communicating Accurately

At one job, I was having some trouble with a customer service rep. There were days she missed appointments with me. There were days that she arrived very late and kept me waiting for meetings. Then, there were days that she didn't arrive at all and I was left to manage the issues without her. These instances happened a lot. In fact, in a one-year time period, her grandmother had died six times and three times her tonsils (which were removed at age 8) caused her to be out sick. Her approach with the people she dealt with was brash and unprofessional. Clearly, there were some problems with this rep.

I realized it was time for me to intervene in this situation. I called her manager. I wanted to explain my concerns in a calm and logical manner and find a solution to the problem.

"Surely this rep can appreciate that arriving to meetings on time helps us know what to expect and how we can count on her," I said.

The manager agreed.

"And *surely the rep* realizes her customers have only a limited amount of patience for the supposed tragedies in her life."

Again, agreement from the manager.

"And I think it is important to mention here that being professional goes a long way when working with people. *Surely the rep* recognizes that if you respect people you have a better chance of being respected."

There was no response from the manager. There was silence on the other end of the phone line. Then, with much confusion in his voice, he said, "Mrs. Dowse, I'm a little puzzled here. According to my records, the customer service rep for your area is Theresa; her name is not *Shirley*."

At first, I was more puzzled than the manager. What was he talking about? Theresa, Shirley? Then it occurred to me what he was thinking. My only response was to simply say, "*S-u-r-e-l-y*" not the *name* Shirley."

It seemed that every time I said, *"Surely the rep,"* he assumed I was calling the customer service rep by her name. Once we established *who* we were talking about and *what* we were talking about, the conversation went much better. As for my problems with *"Shirley the customer service rep,"* they began to look much smaller than the ones I had with her manager!

Having the aptitude to communicate effectively is paramount in any relationship.

Communication (whether verbal or nonverbal) is a simple formula. A message is sent and a message is received. For us humans this transfer of information is where the trouble begins. Individuals have so much baggage and armor that we often distort the signal being sent and the transmission being received.

While I was working with one organization, a manager told me about an individual he was having difficulty communicating with. "I finally figured it out," he said. "Tom is a

56,000 *bps*." He went on to explain that *bps* or bits per second is the rate of speed computers, using modems, transfer information through the telephone lines. The high-pitched screeching sound you hear as you start up your modem is actually the two machines agreeing which *bps* they will use to communicate with each other. A *bps* of 56,000 is sending out information at top rate speed and dumping a great deal of information at one time, while 33,600 *bps* is a slow rate of information exchange. What this manager had discovered while communicating with his employee was that, in order for the message to get through to Tom, he had to talk quickly and give a lot of information at once, otherwise he would lose Tom's attention and interest. Tom enjoyed jumping from topic to topic, dealing with all sorts of information at one time. This naked manager discovered the precise fit to best communicate with this person.

It's up to the naked manager to determine what *bps* or approach will work best when transferring information to another person. We are all different and information does not always process the same way for everyone. People hear, see, and understand messages differently. And then from their individual perspectives, they respond to the message being received based on what they've understood.

The most effective communication results when you first determine how information can best be exchanged. It is foolish to automatically assume that what you've said is what the other person heard. Ashleigh Brilliant writes ,"My great ambition is to secure a speaking part in my own life."[7] Wouldn't it be wonderful to communicate with ease! To evolve beyond misperceptions that contradict the truth! In the real world, however, attaining clear and correct communicated messages takes work.

The ability to communicate in an effective manner is a necessity for managers and often highly challenging. You can possess many skills, but if you lack the ability to communicate effectively your job as a manager has just gotten enormously more difficult. If there is no form of communication between people then there is no connection or alliance. And connection and alliance are fundamental for a manager to possess.

Watch out

Communication takes two forms, verbal and nonverbal. Verbal communication comes out of your mouth, whereas nonverbal communication includes the movement of your hands, arms, eyes, head, feet, and shoulders. Nonverbal communication reflects people's true feelings, their true nakedness. In a study conducted on communication, researchers found that 55% of all the communication sent to another person is done solely through body language—55% percent! That means over half of all the information you send to another person is *not* sent primarily by tone of voice or content. It is being read from your physical appearance and actions. An important question to ask yourself is, "Am I sending out the message I want to send?" "Am I communicating the truth?" If your nonverbal message is overriding your verbal one, the listener might distrust you. The reverse is also true. Ask yourself, "Am I receiving information accurately?" Are you checking to make sure the nonverbal messages match the verbal messages being sent to you?

Here's a quick exercise. Look at your wrist and say the time out loud. Now find a piece of paper and something to write with. *Without looking at your watch again,* draw a picture of your watch face. If you are not wearing a watch, draw a picture of the key pad on your telephone. Go to it!

When you are done, take a look at how you did. While drawing your watch, did you remember:

the brand name?
the second hand?
if the markings were arabic or roman numerals or just lines?

Some people I know draw a round watch face when they have a square watch. If you drew the key pad, did you realize that the numbers 1 and 0 do not have any letters associated with them? Did you know that with some phones Q and Z are not used?

How often do you look at your watch or phone each day? What other things might you be missing and not taking notice of as you go through your day? You may be missing nonverbal clues in the same way. If 55% of our communication is through nonverbal signals, it is important to be alert to the many clues you can receive while communicating. There's a Bible verse that says, "If the blind leads the blind, both shall fall into the ditch." If two people do not communicate well, they may get stuck in a rut or ditch and be lost in linguistic land forever. Naked managers must be alert to all the messages being communicated to them. Careful observation will help determine which *bps* to use in order to communicate accurately!

Naked managers are open and genuine in their approach to communications. They *send out* messages of "what you see is what you get." Both their verbal and nonverbal messages are congruent. They *receive* messages of "I'm willing to be open and hear what you have to say." They do not shut down the communication channels because they assume the message sent is insignificant or contradictory to their viewpoint. As a naked manager, your conversations are not based on your agenda only. Naked managers are aware that personal communication filters exist. They know that the more you are open to the information people have to give, the more information you will receive.

Some managers fear giving up too much information or exposing too much of themselves. In the spirit of an open and genuine approach, naked managers communicate well because of the high level of confidence and comfort they possess. Those fearing open and genuine dialogue retreat, avoid the topic, or redirect the issue as a defense to protect their nakedness or the exposure of their soul. Hawaiians place high regard on how much information can be retrieved non-verbally. They believe that if you maintain eye contact with people you can steal their *mana*, their personal power. For the naked manager, there is no personal power to steal—only power to share. Staying blind from communicated messages will keep you blind from what you need to know.

Listen up

Each of us has been given two ears and one mouth, My best advice is to use them proportionately! Listen more than you speak. In the height of conflict I have been known to tell individuals that "It's okay if your brain stops working; all I ask is that you turn off the volume!"

Humans talk at a rate of 140 words per minute and listen at the rate of 420 words per minute. In other words, while someone is speaking, the listener can go off and take a mental personal vacation while the other person rambles on. Sometimes during these extra moments, the listener's brain is racing to prepare what to say next. In either case, you are not really listening. To be able to listen accurately is a skill, and a wonderful gift to give. When you listen, *really* listen, demonstrating an interest in what the other person is saying, you will discover more than the verbal information he or she has to offer. It is a known fact that the best negotiators are the ones with the most amount of information. Information comes from asking questions to make sure you have listened correctly. When people feel listened to, they become more responsive and open to sharing information. In any organization when more open, valid information is given, communication is less contaminated and misconceptions are less likely to occur.

The goal for a naked manager is to create a dialogue, not a monologue. Remember, resistance begets resistance and not listening begets not listening. Finding out other people's opinions, perspectives, and issues allows you to deal with situations from a greater vantage point. With this essential information you can manage and make decisions more effectively.

THE BUSINESS OF LISTENING

In Business . . .

To listen effectively is to reach a clarity of understanding

To understand clearly is to respond appropriately

To respond appropriately is to enhance communication

To enhance communication is to support cooperation

To support cooperation is to improve morale

To improve moral is to increase job commitment

To increase job commitment is to focus on productivity

Listening is Good Business

(Reprinted with permission. *The Business of Listening.* Bone, Diane; Crisp Publications, 1200 Hamilton Court, Menlo Park, California 94025. 800-442-7477)

Managers have so much information coming at them each day, how can they listen to it all? The answer: by deciphering the messages sent. People communicate using two fundamental elements, content and ego. Content is the actual facts. Ego is the aspects of the person's personality in relation to the content. Even with concentrated listening, managers can confuse content with ego.

"I'm concerned about how we will make the deadline by the 15th."

The ego statement is that "I am concerned," the content is "there is a deadline on the 15th."

"How are we ever going to do this job with only three people?"

The ego statement is that "I am fearful," the content is "big job, few people."

Depending on how you want to direct the conversation, you can focus on the ego or on the content. In conflict situations you will find that people have a difficult time dealing with the content until the ego part is addressed and resolved. When you understand the difference between content and ego, you will be able to decipher what you have heard and respond to it more appropriately.

The following chart provides a simple explanation of the differences between content and ego and some responses you can use in each case.

Communication Elements

Element	Related to	Games Played	Response
Content	• Facts • Specifics • Details • Possibilities • Characteristics	• given in small amounts to keep interest high • given to test if trustworthy • aimed to gain position (information is power)	• Listen • Filter out unnecessary information • Clarify facts and details
Ego	• Values • Self-esteem • Feelings • Motivation • Commitment • Opinions • Interests • Fears • Wants • Needs • Desires	• told for "poor me" effect • to intimidate • to raise self-esteem • to release anger • to pass on problem	• Paraphrase what was heard • Validate what was heard • Clarify the issues • Ask questions to understand the other persons perspective • Invite further exploration

When people don't feel heard, they usually keep repeating the same point over and over. If you do not address the issues of the ego (the part of the person that feels unheard), the person gets stuck and is unable to move to the issue of content. As a listener, keep your senses open for themes and behaviors so you can clarify and respond to what the person is really trying to say.

Linking it together

The illusion of communication is that we believe people have received the message we sent. Part of the problem comes from assuming we are all speaking the same language. Not so! If I were to say the word "puppy," one person might think, "cute little cuddly puppy." Another person might think, "yappy dog that eats your shoes and pees on your rug." The same word, "puppy," can create different perspectives for different people.

I learned this lesson early in my career. I was in charge of creating the camp totem pole. Every day perfectly normal children would attend camp. As soon as they walked onto the premises, they picked right up on the Indian theme and ran around like Custer was about to make his last stand!

One of my camp duties was to get the creative juices flowing by chiseling and painting a 14 foot log to transform it into a totem pole. For many hours many people worked hard on the job. After a month we were finally ready for the finishing touch. To complete the job, we needed to give the totem pole two coats of urethane, a type of very tough outdoor varnish. Now, I realize that we weren't following authentic reproduction procedures, but we wanted a lasting finish so we wouldn't have to do this job again!

I called the camp director at his office. Bob the director wasn't in, but I did reach his secretary Bonnie Lou.

"Bonnie," I said, "would you please ask Bob to bring 48 ounces of urethane when he comes out to camp today. We'll need it to finish working on the totem pole."

Bonnie Lou took the message and I went back to chiseling and painting. When Bob came into the office that day Bonnie Lou gave him my message.

"Bob, Eileen called and she needs you to being 48 ounces of 'your thing' to camp so she can finish building the totem pole."

"My thing?" asked Bob, "What's my thing?"

"Well, everyone knows, Bob, that your thing is bourbon."

Bob arrived at camp at 5 p.m. that evening with a brown paper bag full of "his thing"—48 ounces of bourbon. He handed me the bag with a smirk on his face and said, "I'm sure this will help make it easier to finish the totem pole."

"Thanks, Bob," and I took the bag and opened it. The look on my face was more than puzzled. "Bob, this isn't 48 ounces of urethane!"

"Heck no, it's 48 ounces of 'my thing'. Isn't that what you asked for?"

"Maybe I did?" I was sure that I gave the correct perspective, I just didn't take into account all the other factors for getting my message across. Bob was right though, 'his thing' did make finishing the totem pole easier! And I learned to not assume the communicated message sent is the same as the message that is received.

It is almost as though everyone has a little dance card in their head. When we hear certain messages communicated, memories, ideas, or pictures are generated in our mind and we respond or "dance" to that tune we think we have heard.

The key to communication is understanding the other person's perspective and making sure you both understand what is being said (you are dancing to the same music). Awareness affects the communication interchange, from the initial response to the final outcome.

The following box offers some questions to promote and ensure mutual understanding.

> ## Communicating for Understanding

- **What I understand you to say is** _____
  (to clarify you heard the information correctly)
- **Let's see, the key points are** _____
  (to help you and the speaker organize and remember)
- **You referred to** _____
  Could you tell me what that is? _____
  (to get specific details and content)
- **I had understood you to say** _____
  but now I hear you saying _____
  (to help clear up seeming contradictions)

Communication includes watching and listening to the verbal and nonverbal messages being sent. Essentially what you are doing is establishing an accurate *bps* to use with a person. No matter what communication abilities the other person has, the naked manager's objective is to determine the appropriate approach and message to send. The goal is to send a message so that it can be received. A naked manager understands that communication requires attention and connection. It is going in one ear and *not* out the other.

Solutions from the collective wisdom

- Listen—it's important to learn and practice. (This was the key point made by those surveyed.)
- Give recognition to people and encourage them to speak.
- Give short, clear messages.
- Communicate to instill confidence in yourself and others.
- Stop procrastinating about communicating; if you have something to say—say it.
- Never stop improving on your communication skills.
- Remember to give *appropriate* communication.
- When honesty grows, stress diminishes.
- Set expectations for openness.
- Communicate, reach out, and let someone know that you are listening to him or her.
- People are not willing to listen until they feel heard. Let people have a chance to talk first. It will help them listen better to you.
- If you don't say what you mean, then you will not mean what you say.
- Don't assume you heard it right the first time. *Say* what you think you heard and check to make sure you got it right.
- In order to encourage honesty and openness, be honest and open yourself.
- Mirror how you want people to communicate with you—role model good communication behavior.

- Let other people finish speaking instead of finishing their sentences for them.

- Call for truth.

- Go directly to the source that communicated the message—it is less distorted that way.

- As soon as you know there is a problem, bitching to someone else doesn't accomplish a solution. Go and talk to the person you have the problem with.

- What someone has to say can be as important as what you have to say. So listen up!

- There's usually a reason why people need to tell you something. Look deeper for the meaning of messages.

- Separate emotions from logic in a conversation. Decide what you want to focus on and go in that direction.

8

Natural Instincts
Using Your Intuition

The naked truth is that everyone has the ability to be intuitive. It is a natural instinct and part of our biological makeup. You have a physical body with physical attributes, systems, and responses. You also have a spiritual body with emotions, knowledge, ethereal attributes, and intuition. "The really valuable thing is intuition," according to Albert Einstein.[8] Together these physical and spiritual components make up your total self.

All creatures in the animal kingdom have natural instincts or talents they use to respond to environmental stimulants. Animals use different senses to protect themselves from danger and to survive. Creatures use an amazing array of styles of intuition, each one appropriate to their situation.

A dolphin determines if objects are friend or foe by decoding sound waves through an echolocation system. Bats determine the location and properties of an object by using the sensory cells in their brains to interpret echoes. Sharks, using their noses, pick up a weak electrical stimulus to detect the presence of their prey. And birds instinctively know to fly in the calm eye of a hurricane for safety and protection.

In all creatures the brain picks up sensations from the environment and assesses the cues and clues it receives. This use of the senses is the process of instinct. Intuition is purest form of instinct. Intuition helps people respond to situations in their lives, independent of experience or reason.

I admit that logical and analytical thinking are necessary in life, yet they are not the only components for determining behavior or making decisions. Acute perceptions, precognition, and ingenious wisdom occur when you use your instincts, intelligence, or intuition. In Buddhism, intuition is considered "intellectual light." The Latin word for "intuition" is related to keen vision or insight. Whatever the meaning, intuition is a natural ability *not* found at a conscious level that is too often disregarded. Intelligence can only analyze; intuition is the absolute in brain power, the unified working of the right and left hemispheres of the brain. Intuition is the basis of all life and thought and works at a superconscious level. Think of intuition as the divining rod for the unconscious.

Intuition is not mystical bunk or an evil phenomenon. It won't tell you exactly when and where things are going to happen—that is paranormal activity. Intuition is simply having the solution without knowing all the details. It's using your brain, the spiritual component of your being, to make choices in the immediate moment and obtain insights in your life.

For a long time I was confused about intuition. I knew I had it and I knew I used it. My approach and experiences seemed different from those of other people I spoke to. I realized that just as we all have different learning styles to retrieve information and obtain knowledge, we also have different intuitive styles to choose from. You might notice that the intuitive styles I present here have great similarities to other learning styles and communication approaches.

In my research it was interesting to discover that intuitive styles have many similarities to the theories of neurolinguistic programming (using your nervous system, the mental pathways for the five senses, combined with language for more effective communication and changes in behavior). And why not? We all have preferred styles of doing things. Why should intuition be any different. Most people have a preferred approach and often are unaware that they have other intuition options.

The following is a list of intuitive approaches from Pete Sanders Jr., a MIT-trained scientist who has done extensive work in the area of intuition and brain power. He offers four ways for people to tap into their intuitive resources. (some bear similarity to the dolphin, bat, shark, and bird).[9]

Auditory—Do you hear yourself saying, *"A little voice told me* and I knew what to do?"* You have an auditory intuitive style. You listen for the clues. Those little voices will pop into your head from who knows where and actually tell you the idea or concept.

Visual—Can you see the solution? If you have a *"clear picture or vision"* of what needs to be done, you are the visually intuitive person. You can see how the outcome or event will transpire. From that picture, you develop a plan, approach, and attitude.

Kinetic—Perhaps you get *"a gut feeling about this one."* There is a sensation in your stomach and you know how to respond to an event. You obtain your intuitive insights kinetically, by the feeling you get from your body sensations.

Cognitive—Do you *"just know it's the right thing to do?"* You are a strongly cognitive person. Every fiber in your being knows that it's the right thing. You can't explain it, you just *know* it is.

Since we are all different, it seems logical to assume that our intuitive styles can vary as well. This is another reason why it is so hard for people to accept and believe this natural human ability. Yet all of us have the ability to be intuitive. The key to using your intuition is to use the approach that you are most comfortable with, the approach that best taps into your natural ability.

Listen to your little voice. Don't confuse that gut feeling with indigestion. Believe and honor your daydreams and visions. Be comfortable with that overwhelming sense of knowing without having all the facts. There is no logical path to these natural laws—validity comes from within. In fact, if you need another person to validate your intuitions in order to accept them, then your ability to intuit is skewed. Clear intuition requires the ability to respect your own impressions.

Intuitive Managers

In this rapidly changing world, intuition is quickly becoming the single most important characteristic of managers. It is the tool that most profoundly affects change. It's a jungle out there and the need for using intuition is on the rise. Animals survive best in the jungle by intuition and instinct. Why not you? Managers are working in environments where from time to time they may feel vulnerable, confused, and naked. When lowered to this primal level, you begin to rely on your inner resources and your natural instincts, making good decisions with incomplete information. I call this the Indiana Jones approach, "making it up as you go along." In the Indiana Jones movie series, Harrison Ford plays an adventurous archaeologist who very often has no other choice but to use his intuition to save himself from predicaments.

For the naked manager situations involving risk and uncertainty are the ones where intuition is most often used. Using your intuition will help you be innovative, creative, and, with confidence, boldly go where no one has gone before. This ability to deal with ambiguity, implausibility, and uncertainty is actually key to using your intuition. Often when you are "just making it up as you go along" you get there just fine because you relied on intuition.

In Carl Jung's Myers Briggs Type Indicator personality test, only 25% of the general population reports a preference for intuition. The other 75% prefer immediate, real, solid facts and are not often inspired. It is odd that something that is so natural, intuition, is not the style of choice. Perhaps the reason is that intuition cannot be easily proven or justified. Intuition is often discounted as an unexplained thought rather than acute perception gained from the brain. For naked managers, justifying intuition is not an issue because they know not everything has to make sense and be explained. Intuition may not be quantifiable, yet few deny its existence. If everything had to first make sense, the world might never have seen the light bulb, the telephone, or the Internet.

Top-level executives must rely on intuition, along with logic, to take their companies to the leading edge. As you rise to higher levels in your organization, the risks and demands placed on you greatly increase. In addition, you also have less time to respond to situations. Managers and employees in the 21st century are all being pushed for maximum output. You know what happens when you push people too hard? They begin to use their primary instinct, intuition. Nobody who rises to a high level in an organization does so without the use of intuition. The brilliant few who run the organization are there because they have the instinct and brilliance to do it. Intuition is the spark that leads to success, and it plays a key role in any thought and discovery. Naked managers understand this way of thinking and use it to their advantage.

Ingenious solutions don't evolve slowly from deductions. Constant assessment causes paralysis by analysis. Intuition is the capacity to take ideas and make them reality. As an intuitive manager you must be both passionate and sensitive. To be passionate is to be intuitive about concepts. To be sensitive is to be intuitive about people. When these qualities are combined, the manager can understand what is important and implement what needs to be done. Your intuition is an important strategic planning tool for maximizing performance and success.

Not all intuition is good

In the world of management, using intuition is not always positive. Strongly intuitive people can come packaged with a strong ego. They rely solely on their intuition and believe that whatever they say is right and they certainly don't need any facts to make decisions. This naive overconfidence causes them to think they are god's gift to executive management. They can often be found going into an abstract tyrant role where the words they speak are like stone tablets. They have delusions of grandeur, feeding on the power of their intuitive self. It is impossible to convince these people that your thoughts have validity too. A word of caution is needed while relying on your intuition. As with everything in life, have balance. Use intuition in relation to your other abilities. You were given many skills and talents, so use them all well.

Relying on intuition

There are times that you may become discouraged with your intuitive abilities. The "little voice" may have given you the wrong message. Or that "gut feeling" may have proven to be the wrong approach. Remember, intuition comes from your unconscious. As they say in computer language, your problem may be a "systems error." More simply put, you might not be listening to yourself correctly and using a compatible network. The intuitive messages you are getting might be wishful thinking or distortions caused by fears, memories, and impressions stored in your mind. The solution to this dilemma is quieting your mind and allowing time for reflection. I'm not talking about the "drive through" approach of deciding what you want to reflect on—think about it for 15 minutes and the move on. No, I'm referring to releasing that brain sludge that is clouding up your thinking and opening your mind to possibilities, opening up your spiritual body. The spiritual deals with emotions, knowledge, ethereal elements, and intuition. Einstein said, "Why is it I get my best ideas shaving in the morning?"[10] Why? Because he gave his mind a chance to open up and let his subconscious integrate through different inputs. I personally get my best ideas at 70 mph. I now carry a tape recorder in my car, I have found it safer to speak into the mike than write it down on the interstate! If you want to use your intuition, you need to be open and willing to be receptive to what your unconscious wants you to know.

There have been some studies done on how environmental factors can enhance or inhibit intuition. If you want to create the ultimate surroundings for intuitive thought, supply the following to the room you do your thinking in:

- paint the room with light colors, in natural tones

- have it lit with natural sunlight

- have the temperature set between 70 and 73 degrees Fahrenheit

- set humidity between 60 and 70 percent

- have relaxing music playing—it helps trigger memories and lets the right and left brain hemispheres work better together

- have some plants; they keep the air clean and decrease irritating pollution

It is hard to be intuitive when you are overtired, stressed out about things, or your emotional state is charged to jump at every detail. If you are going to listen to what your inside has to say, you need to quiet yourself to reach the unconscious part of your mind.

Ways to exercise your intuition

The following is a list of ways to enhance your natural intuitive abilities. Enjoy them, play with them, give them a try.

1. **Sleep on it:** When you are faced with an issue, sleep on it and take your dreams seriously. Thomas Edison used dreams to solve his problems. Write your dreams down on paper when you wake up and refer to your notes later when you are thinking about solutions. If you give your conscious mind a chance to shut down during sleep, your unconscious mind can move in and give you intuitive clues. If you are dreaming you are sleeping, and it is much easier to work out issues when you are rested.

2. **Day dream:** Let your mind wander to wherever it wishes to go while you are awake. Find time and surroundings to day dream in (take a walk in the woods, listen to music, stare out a window). Let your brain go in whatever direction it desires. *NOTE: daydreaming can be hazardous to your health if done at times that require your full concentration. Use only in safe environments.*

3. **Take notes.** Write your hunches and thoughts down (it doesn't matter on what, if an old receipt is handy, use it). If you have access to the electronic world, "'speak into' the microphone, please." It would be awful to miss an intuitive flash for lack of remembering it.

4. **Play intuitive games.**
    *   When the phone rings, guess who's calling before you answer it.

- Imagine who will walk into the room next; think about what they are wearing and what they are carrying and the mood they are in.

- Predict the card a person is holding without seeing it.

- Roll some dice and guess what numbers will come up.

5. **Listen.** Close your eyes, open your mind, and listen for the first word that pops into your mind. No matter how bizarre, use that word as the "theme for the day." When situations arise think of that word before you begin to deal with them.

6. **Tingle.** Tap into sensations your body experiences, when you meet people. What instinctive message is your mind or body giving you?

All things are energy ($E = MC^2$). Objects are a dynamic power and can take on different forms. They can be neither created nor destroyed. Energy can be neither created nor destroyed; energy can only change in form. According to this universally accepted theory, the book you are reading is energy, the chair you are sitting in is energy, *you* are energy. The question I ask you is what will you do with your energy, use it or suppress it? What will you do with your natural intuition, use it or deny it? You have the energy to make things happen. Know yourself and listen to natural instincts. This is the naked edge for success in business!

Solutions from the collective wisdom

- Give yourself time to listen to what your body tells you.
- Meditate—it gives you time to get yourself settled and puts things in perspective.
- Have faith in your instincts—you really have them.
- Keep yourself healthy; it makes it easier for your instincts to work.
- Don't believe that you have to think like everyone else—that sense you have is more reliable than friends.
- Trust your own instincts—you are the one that will have to live with the decisions.
- Be persistent; it's not easy for everyone to see the vision and feel the urgency.
- Expect to have intuition.
- Be open and things will come to you.
- Observe how other people are making decisions.
- Don't only think with your head, think with your heart.
- Take time to play—it clears your mind.
- Choose friends and colleagues who can realign and change your energy.
- Find religion—it can give you strength and wisdom needed for the job.
- Keep balance in your life; it is too easy to get out of whack.

9

That's the Spirit
Spirituality in the Workplace

This was a difficult chapter for me to write. I knew the topic was important for the naked manager, yet I didn't know how to form the words to give its message magnitude. I remember getting some brilliant concepts for this chapter flying at 10,000 feet in a DC9. I began madly scratching out notes on the only thing I could find, a barf bag (and even then space was limited because I could only write on the outside since the inside was wax-coated). I created five bags of ideas, which I share with you now.

> *As a side note . . . if you think spirituality is hard to talk about, try explaining to the stewardess why you need so many barf bags for the flight. "Please help me. The ideas are coming out and I need something to catch them in!"*

Talking about spirituality in business can be a taboo topic. It requires political savvy, extraordinary alertness, and exquisite timing. Why? Because not everyone on this planet is ready to or wants to hear about the spiritual aspects of life.

Long ago if you acted or alluded to believing something spiritually different than the norm, you would have been burned at the stake. Now in the age of asbestos, it is thought that people talking about spirituality, outside the walls of worship, either show up at your door wearing suits and riding bicycles or look like hippies speaking about new age, new movements, and new moons. People acknowledge that spirituality has a place, in a church or a foxhole, but *not* in a business.

I was personally challenged by how I could appropriately address the issue of spirituality in business. In my quest, I became president of the advisory board for a nonprofit organization called Spirit in Business. The group offers monthly programs and resources to anyone interested in attending. I thought by hanging out with business professionals interested in this topic, I could understand the role spirituality plays in organizations.

I wanted desperately to understand how to speak of spirituality without having people run away or shut down when the topic came up. I chose to enter Duke Divinity School and study, practice, and experience the role of hospital chaplain to see how it affected people's lives.

When I talked to people from both of these areas, their answers and responses varied.

- *"My work is sucking my soul dry. So I started to look at how I can start to feel better in life and feel better about my integrity and purpose."*

- *"As vice president, my company has grown from 18 to 8,000 in 3 years and the entrepreneurial spirit is starting to be squashed. I want to know how to get the spirit back into my workplace."*

- *"I'm sure glad I have my spiritual side right now in my life. It's the only thing keeping me focused to get through this mess."*

- *"I'm spiritual, not religious and I get my strength from my beliefs."*

- *"My body and mind are beaten up in this job, but they're not going to get my spirit. It's my spirit that will get me through."*

- *"I may be a one of the top executives here, but if I'm going to start working well at this job I have to be truthful and honest about who I am. I've decided to document what kind of person I really am and where I am in life. I'm not going to live a falsehood in my mind anymore. It's time to gain some integrity. I'm meeting my spirit and saying, 'Let's dance.' It's time for me to get it together and start working more effectively from my heart."*

Each person I spoke to consistently talked about his or her spirit as the inner strength or inner power from which he or she could draw from. Their spiritual side is essentially managing their entire life and is critical to their existence.

I noticed, that the concept of spirituality came more easily to people in crisis. They were more open to accessing their inner strength, out of necessity to cope. Everyone I spoke with, whether they were open to the concept of spirituality or not, placed great importance on their inner power, their natural resources—in essence to their spirituality.

People know there is a spiritual part within them; they just aren't comfortable talking about it in work situations. My experience with Spirit in Business and hospital chaplaincy enlightened me to one thought: the basis of spirituality is simple and is twofold.

1. Spirituality has a vital role in our existence.

2. Spirituality's form is different, just as people are.

The *S*-word, "spirituality," is often confused with the *R*-word, "religion." Fundamental differences between religion and spirituality are:

Religion is external, seeking outward expression.
It is about

- ceremonies

- rites

- scriptures

- methods for worship

- belonging to a group

Spirituality is internal, operating from an inner presence
It is about

- having personal awareness

- having direction of purpose

- practicing universal values

- extending help to others

- experiencing inner happiness

Spirit is the internal power in people and organizations that generates the principles and practices of:

- achieving a sense of worth

- creating direction of purpose

- offering clarity of judgment

- operating with integrity

- providing compassion, openness, and collaboration

This internal power isn't judged on whether it is good or evil, but rather on how it is issued. If you consistently work from an external power source, you are not using your spirit, you are protecting and feeding your ego. For the naked manager, bringing the internal power of spirituality into your profession means dealing with the methods for creating harmony in your work environment and in your interpersonal relationships. It also means being conscious that others have a spirit as well.

In the Buddhist faith, if you are a spiritual warrior you have the courage to be different. This is much like showing off "birthmarks" for the naked manager. It means you have the ability to recognize who you really are, and have the motivation to continually become.

Mother Theresa didn't believe that spirituality had to with talking *at* a person. "There should be less talk. A preaching point is not a meeting point."[11] Spirituality for her was when thoughts were converted into actions. For the naked manager, it is removing the "big but," exposing yourself and working with a pure heart. Being spiritual is letting the natural power evolve within each of us, and be used for compassion, openness and collaboration.

For a manager to promote religious concepts at work can be dangerous. The legal department might show up at your door reciting excerpts from the constitution, employee rights, or court dates. At the same time, organizations are making a shift to more spiritual approaches to deal with employee needs. Businesses are offering services to enhance interpersonal relationships, ways to balance life and work, and methods to promote wellness. Good business practices are beginning to recognize the importance of having concern for the well-being of their human resources as well as their production resources. The aspect of spirituality helps to make sense out of life and helps people find a peaceful home and refuge within their being.

Unfortunately, making sense can be for all the wrong reasons. I have a friend who never was very religious. His father on the other hand was a devout Jew and always wished his son would be closer to the faith. While father and son were very close, this difference in beliefs was the one area they could never agree on. This past year my friend's father died at the age of 95. His son, in his 60's, was deeply affected by the loss of a long time friend and parent. He had great difficulty dealing with the closure of this part of his life. He felt the void his father's death had left.

I recently visited my friend for the weekend. It had been six months since the loss of his father. When he picked me up at the airport, I noticed he was wearing a yarmulke, a small circular cap worn by men as a symbol of the Jewish faith. I was very surprised. Here was a man who had never indicated any sign of religious belief before, publicly showing his faith. I instantly thought how proud his father would have been to see his son standing in an airport wearing a yarmulke. I could only deduce that the devastation of his father's death had caused him to search and discover the Jewish faith.

"John, what's with the yarmulke?" I asked. "After all these years, have you finally discovered how good religion can be for you?"

John slowly raised his hand to the back of his head, rubbing his yarmulke. "Yup, it seemed to be the right time and the thing I need."

I felt like I was witnessing a conversion in the making. This was amazing. Here was someone who wouldn't be involved in the Jewish faith, now embracing its benefits.

"Well, I'm getting older, Eileen; time and experience have changed me, and this was just the right thing to do; it made sense."

At this point John removed the yarmulke of fine needlework from his head, and bent down to show me the back of his head. He spoke with great conviction and devotion and said, "This was my father's yarmulke and now I wear it because it hides my bald spot perfectly! It works for me! See it's a perfect fit!"

People use religious beliefs for a variety of reasons (as I discovered!). These religious rites and methods of worship are not the focus of this chapter.

What this chapter describes is "spirituality" not "religion." It refers to the components of life that incorporate intelligence, personality, self-consciousness, will, and the methods for nurturing the spirit within you. It is about how to bring intention and integrity to work.

Moving toward spirituality

While I was talking about the issue of spirituality at work, one president of an organization told me, "Eileen, people build so many levels of crud at work. I think, at this point in the game, we have got to create opportunities in work situations where, if there is a crack in the crud, no matter how small, we have to help employees have a chance to break out. Otherwise we will lose very good people". This is the role of the naked manager; create opportunities for yourself and your employees to have life come out and become a more dynamic force. Are you and your staff working and living to the extent you have nerve enough to? Or has the "crud" consumed you and limited your abilities?

Realizing work can suffocate the essence of a person from within, naked managers can find opportunities to retrieve the potential in all of us, thus increasing operations. When naked managers don't recognize the spiritual part of a person, they have seriously underutilized this asset in themselves and their organizations. They will be working with spirit deprivation.

I am thrilled to see that some organizations are making the shift toward whole-person management and spirit-filled organizations. I believe this is occurring primarily because individuals are determining what they want from their work environment. Four major changes are influencing this transition:

1. **Workplaces are becoming frightening environments.** People feel insecure, frightened, and vulnerable. They are looking for help in managing these new feelings.

2. **The workforce is graying.** Baby boomers are growing old. They are beginning to find work less satisfying and sustaining. As they take stock of their lives, they are beginning to slow down and let go of the trivial. They are focusing more on how to feel good about and within themselves.[12]

3. **The supportive role and influence of churches and civic groups is declining.** The basic human need for belonging and association is being derived from work environments. Work is beginning to take on the role of providing the only consistent link for people.

4. **Knowledge of spiritual alternatives has increased with access to information.** Interest in Eastern philosophies is prompting people to investigate new options for understanding their place in the world. The Internet, physical displays of Eastern religions, and alternate beliefs are increasingly accessible in North America. This broadening of perspective is helping people to

   - expand their thinking

   - create opportunities to examine the true nature of physical existence; and

   - end some illusions of identity

These four changes are affecting the way managers need to manage in today's corporate climate. For the naked manager, spirituality is the ultimate in nakedness. Employees and businesses are beginning to realize that technology cannot solve all business problems. The spiritual principles of loyalty, openness, honesty, and collaboration are where managers must focus to enhance their work environments. The language to get to these points might be different. The focus here is on the principles and values for persons and their spirits. When you can find and manifest your spiritual core, effectiveness and attainment begin to happen. Naked managers are grounded in the belief that purpose and hope exist in their ability to guide employees.

I once spoke to a group of 220 accountants about how to be creative and resolve conflict. (It was a challenging group!) One person sat in the front row and took it upon himself to be the heckler. He disagreed with everything I said, challenged every word I spoke, and was beginning to make my life miserable. I called an early break and went over to speak with this person, hoping to use my best naked manager approach.

"You seem to know a lot about this topic."

"Oh yeah, I've taken some courses, and I even know some mediators like yourself."

"Is that right? Who do you know?"

"Sam Long."

"You know Sam? Unbelievable! I know Sam. He's a great guy. We do a lot of work together. He is so easy to like and you just want to be in his presence. When we work together, it's wonderful. How do you know Sam?"

"He married my ex-wife."

Then I understood what was happening. His spirit was hurt, and I was in the line of fire. We talked about the anger and distaste he had for Sam and mediators in general.

By inviting this person to get open and mentally naked, he was able to look deeper at his damaged spirit. I was able to shift the relationship from combative to collaborative. I touched a point that allowed him to acknowledge why he was not at peace, and opened a conversation to help him deal with it. Naked management is about making a safe place to get vulnerable. Openness is spirit building. A naked manager's job is to create situations to help souls shine, not fester.

Part of a naked manager's mission is be human with his or her own humanness. Be responsible for your actions. By being less human you are being less spiritual. By being more human you can build trust, closeness, and a strong sense of interdependency. The world of business has become less human and less spiritual. What's happening in your organization? Are you missing opportunities for having joy at work because you are not human?

One of the issues that gets in way of spirit is ego. Employees and organizations can have big egos that are not healthy. Being open and practicing the human traits of humbleness, compassion, and honesty help move mind-sets toward the spiritual, toward working from the heart.

The concept of being a naked manager is to get rid of the ego as a motivating factor in your actions. When you work from a spirit-filled place rather than from your ego point, you increase tranquillity and understanding of purpose.

Guided by your ego

Your ego deals with protecting you from fear and vulnerability. Your ego analyzes, condemns, denies, evaluates, interprets, and judges almost everything. When you witness things that repulse you, your ego side is challenged to justify your thinking. When you see traits you admire, the envious side of the ego makes you feel less, without and wanting.

Guided by your spirit

Your spirit deals with experiencing life with openness, connectives, and integrity. Spirituality isn't about dealing with all-powerful beings. It focuses on inner awareness and attributes for living each day, with ourselves and with the people we meet.

It is sometimes hard to find the spirit within. I heard a comment once from one manager who said, "Where I work it's a slimy, political snakepit." The need to protect your ego can seem to be the only alternative. The thought of letting go

Take a moment to think about it.

Directions

1. List five things important to you.
2. Rank-order them
3. Look at your typical week and list the items you spend the most time on.
4. Assign a percentage to the work devoted in these areas.
5. Are the items you listed in #1 incongruent with your percentages in #4?

The purpose of this question is to assess if you are in balance. Are you using the power of your spirit well?

Other questions to ponder:

- What do you think is worth striving for?
- How would you define what your spirituality is about?
- What is your purpose?
- How is what you are doing related to your spiritual beliefs?
- How is your spirit feeling right now?
- Is your internal power too exhausted to function?
- Are you making decisions to protect only yourself and the mental thoughts that possess you?
- Are you open or closed to the outside world?

Give yourself a spiritual assessment every once and awhile. It would be a shame to be working without all your faculties.

and showing your real self gives way to protecting, comforting, and saving your psyche from danger. Again I ask, "Are you living your life to the extent you have nerve enough to do it?" Are you functioning from your ego state or spirit? When people move past protecting their inner self and working from their natural internal power, their spirit becomes alive and at peace to work on anything they want.

Speaking of spirituality

When managers get naked and broach the topic of spirituality, it can be uncomfortable. If you really get spirit into your work environment, there are times it will seem uncomfortable. You might think, "I don't like it. It's not going to work." If you are *not* on the edge, you're probably not doing it.

It is easy to do "safe social chitchat." People want dialogue that is

- safe

- nonintrusive

- non competitive

- well within their comfort zone.

Addressing spiritual issues in the workplace requires some adeptness. Not everyone is able to be open to the subject and value its importance. It all begins with establishing a trusting, truthful environment for yourself and your organization.

As with any initial contact, the process begins with listening to understand, flexibility, patience, and spontaneity. One of my colleague says, *"I won't talk about angels, I won't talk about guides, but I will talk about my spirit. That's what helps me deal with day to day issues."*

If people have trouble relating to the concept of spirituality try, equating it with the heart. "What does your heart say?" "Put your heart into it." "Are you a heartfelt person?" The concept is the same, the words are different. Remember, spirituality is not about religious language. Spiritual language is about relationships with self and others. By using spirituality language and actions you can:

- achieve a sense of worth

- create a direction of purpose

- provide the potential for compassion, openness, and collaboration

How to bring spirituality into the workplace

When people come to work they are not just bodies; their spirits also walk through the door. I can tell when an organization is spirit-deprived. I will hear comments like:

- *"This group has reached rock bottom and has started to dig."*

- *"We can't allow this employee to breed."*

- *"They're not a has-been, they're definitely a won't be."*

- *"Don't listen to them. Their brain stopped working years ago."*

- *"That guy sets low standards and consistently fails to achieve them."*

- *"We hope she goes far—the sooner she starts, the better."*

- *"This employee is depriving a village somewhere of an idiot."*

The purpose of emphasizing spirituality in the workplace is to increase awareness of the universal principles that help people work together more peacefully and productively. The principles that guide a spirit-filled workplace include:

1. **Possessing freedom to express oneself honestly and openly**
   - Establish environments so employees can contribute their wisdom and experience to feel connected to the organization.

2. **Integrating congruency between the inner person and outer environment.**
   - Attempt to understand what employees need and how they can best work in their surroundings.

3. **Respecting others and valuing their differences, strengths and weaknesses**
   - Achieve this in all situations, not only when it is easy to do.

4. **Being considerate of others' needs and desires**
   - People rarely do things for *your* reasons. When you understand their issues, you can work toward mutual gain.

5. **Promoting an emphasis on growth and learning**
   - An organization that is stagnant soon smells and acts like a swamp.

6. **Accepting ownership for one's personal and professional styles**
   - When the focus is on blaming, the energy is on destruction

7. **Encouraging flexible attitudes**
   - "If you always do what you've always done, then you'll always get what you've always got."

8. **Allowing laughter, joy, and playfulness**
   - It will increase creativity, productivity, morale, satisfaction, and retention.

9. **Recognizing the benefits of emotional and intellectual components in life**
   - Allow people to work from both their hearts and their heads; both are necessary for attaining real value.

10. **Creating a physical environment conducive to performance (privacy, lighting, air quality)**
    - The physical, mental, and spiritual components of your body are sensitive to their surroundings. When you enhance the environment, you enhance the person.

(designed by the organization "Spirit in Business" in Research Triangle Park, NC)

Bringing spirit into the workplace includes being human at work. One hard working, successful, well-paid manager I met said, *"The best people I've ever worked with and felt completely comfortable with, were from a group I attended with Al Anon* (the organization for families of alcoholics). *These people were real people."*

As I tried to understand, the person explained, *"That group of people are at a place in their life where they're comfortable with themselves. They don't have to prove something. They're speaking from their core, from their heart. They have nothing to prove. They didn't really have a lot of pride to flaunt around. It is so great to be with real people who aren't pretending they're something they're not."*

This group of individuals was at that point where they could finally take off the masks, cover-ups, and denials they had used for so long to survive. They were now comfortable enough to deal with the present, and say, *"This is* who *I am. This is* what *I'm about."* Protective layers can stunt your growth and hinder you from moving forward. Some people might respond to this story by saying, "Yeah, right Eileen, it's just another Kum Bah Yah moment for a bunch of people, let's deal with the real world." That is the ego talking, not the spirit. I can't emphasize to you enough the benefits that come when you work from the heart and with integrity.

Ways to uplift the spirit with integrity

Developing your spiritual side will offer you a strength both on and off the job. Optimal ability is created when you are willing to stretch your comfort zone and try new things. When Candace Gayle, a speaker from Wilmington, North Carolina, presents her topic on "Spirituality and Business" she has the group participate in a potent exercise. One member of the group is asked to stand up at the front of the room. He or she is instructed to close his or her eyes and extend the right arm, perpendicular to the body. The rest of the audience is told of two options, one of which will be chosen. The instructions to the audience are: I will hold up a finger while standing behind this person standing at the front indicating which option I want you to mentally concentrate on and repeat over and over again in your mind. Address your focus toward this person at the front.

The first option:
"I like you. I can support you."

The second option:
"I don't like you. I won't support you."

For two minutes when the group sends the mental message of *"I like you. I can support you."* the person standing at the front of the room (who is unaware of which option the room has chosen) raises an arm. When the group sends the mental message of *"I don't like you. I won't support you,"* the person's arm lowers. I can assure you I didn't believe it till I saw it for myself.

You possess a great inner power to affect other people. Your inner power is what you believe you are holding in your mind. In relation to this exercise, I ask, Are thoughts draining your energy and prohibiting you from having a human experience? How will you choose to manifest your power, your spirit, as you work with others to promote the universal principles of caring, compassion, collaboration, and integrity? There isn't a formal initiation to becoming spiritual. Your initiation is drawn from relationships.

To uplift your spirit doesn't mean being eccentric, having your thoughts in la-la land, or sitting quietly in the lotus position for hours in order to hear your internal voice speak to you. Uplifting your spirit does mean creating any opportunities to:

- look within

- become aware

- be more purposeful

- gain an inner sense of happiness

- find places and activities to stay alive

- work from a place of truth and goodness

Some spirit-enhancing ideas

- Decorate with flowers and take time to smell them
  —appreciate life

- Look out a window and allow your mind to wander
  —it gives the spirit a chance to surface

- Take a walk and stop along the way
  —changing your environment can change your view of things

- Say hello and smile at people
  —smiling uses less muscles and has a greater effect on others

- Be still for a moment or two
  —breathe in and out and assess how you feel at the moment

- Have a comfortable chair to sit in
    —be good to your soul and bottom!

- Be open in your dealings with people
    —containing with your spirit will only suffocate it

- Laugh out loud
    —it's good for you and it can be contagious

- Wonder about stuff
    —life is full of possibilities

- Give up worry, guilt, and shame
    —work from the spirit not the ego

- Don't forget the "magic word," thank you
    —people matter

- Use crayons
    —your spirit needs trips down memory lane

- If you fall down, pick yourself up, dust yourself off, and start all over again
    —it's okay to make mistakes, it's part of humanness

- Get excited and give yourself permission to be silly
    —share your energy

- Listen to music
    —it opens your physical and mental state to allow thoughts to enter

- Make friends
    —some are silver and some are gold

- Wave to children on school buses
    —positively affect others' lives

- Send thank you notes
    —positively affect others' lives

- "Don't look down on someone unless you are helping them up"
  —Chuck Davis, African American Dancers,
  Durham, North Carolina

- Do anything that brings more:
  —happiness, celebration, relaxation, communication, health, love, joy, creativity, pleasure, abundance, grace, self-esteem, courage, balance, spontaneity, passion, peace, beauty, and life energy to all humans and beings of this planet

Remember, as a naked manager:

It's never too late to have a happy spirit.
Make sure that others do too!

10

Closing the Book on It
Some Final Thoughts

If you think the concepts in this book are a load of bunk or are fine on paper but won't work in reality, then I challenge you to examine your surroundings and your approach to life and management. We all have choices in life, no matter how locked in or unfair we think they may be. You *have* a choice. I saw a sign at a southern fruit stand once; it read, "Our choice 50 cents, your choice 75 cents." Making wise choices is not always easy; it takes work and commitment. You have the choice to change the way you work with people. Change is simply a renewal of energy.

In the preceding chapters I have proposed that keeping an open mind, understanding another person's perspective, staying motivated, letting people know you exist, and being proud of who you are choices that yield the greatest results. These are the skills that hold the greatest value for managers today. Managers need to make hard choices in the current work environment. They must be able to stand up for themselves, take risks, and be willing to be "naked" (metaphorically speaking, of course!). Fostering these attitudes and attributes brings out the best in an individual. Freedom comes from removing masks. You are at your best when you act from your heart and your soul. My advice: tell the truth, tell what you believe is right, and be open to possibilities. With this credo you will never go wrong.

The true power of a manager comes from the ability to handle management without masks and superficial layers. These masks and cover-ups may enhance your look to superiors, it does not help with those you work with. They will know that you are not being honest and trustworthy. Lacking these qualities begins a downward spiral for lack of respect and support. Psychotherapist Jack Kornfield, author of *A Path With Heart,* says "The compartments we create to shield us from what we fear exact their toll later in life."[13]

I consider stress and crisis an opportunity to show what's important to you. As a manager you are a role model who can demonstrate acceptable behaviors. Plato said, "Those having torches will pass them on to others."[14] What is important to you? What do you represent? What are your core issues? What is your wardrobe comprised of, birthday suits or cover-ups? Be conscious of what you believe and why.

The thoughts in this book stress: be what you truly are and hold on to higher principles. Garments are the clothing of the body and opinions and thoughts are the clothing of the mind. It is time to take off the clothing, value your unique abilities and the abilities of others, and be wonderful in your nakedness. Remember, it is ugliness we try to hide, not beauty and wonder. It is time to be whole. When you are naked you reveal yourself. This is what it means to be an honest, authentic, and a true person, comfortable with self. You have the choice to be wonderful.

Notes

1. Dawna Marova, *Open Mind*. (Berkeley: Conari Press, 1996), 118.
2. Ashleigh Brilliant, *Pot-Shot*. (Santa Barbara, 1982), #2471.
3. Robert Ewen, *An Introduction to Theories of Personality*. (New York, San Francisco, London: Academic Press [a subsidiary of Harcourt Brace Jovanovich, Publishers], 1980), 73-74.
4. Dr. Laurence Peter, *Peter's Quotations*. (New York: Bantam Books, 1977), 60.
5. Price Stern Sloan, *The First Really Important Survey of American Habits*. (Los Angeles, Price Stern Sloan, Inc., 1989), 98.
6. Robert Ewen, *An Introduction to Theories of Personality*. (New York, San Francisco, London: Academic Press [a subsidiary of Harcourt Brace Jovanovich, Publishers], 1980), 358.
7. Ashleigh Brilliant, *Pot-Shot*. (Santa Barbara, 1982), #2406.

8. Colin Rose and Malcolm J. Nicholl, *Accelerated Learning for the 21st Century*. (New York: Delacorte Press, 1997), 227.

9. Pete A. Sanders, Jr., *You Are Psychic*. (New York: a Fawcett Columbine Book published by Ballantine Books, 1989), 12.

10. Michael Ray and Rochelle Myers, *Creativity in Business*. (New York: Doubleday, 1986), 137.

11. Dawna Marova, *Open Mind*. (Berkeley: Conari Press, 1996), 12.

12. As referenced by Harry Moody and David Carroll, *The Five Stages of the Soul*. (New York: Anchor Books Doubleday, 1997), 28.

13. Jack Kornfield, *A Path With Heart*. (New York: Bantam Books, 1993), 193.

14. Priec Pritchett, *Firing Up Commitment During Organizational Change, A Handbook for Managers*. (Dallas: Pritchett & Associates, Inc., 1994), 30.

References

Print Materials

Brilliant, Ashleigh. *Pot-Shot*. Santa Barbara, 1982.

Ewen, Robert. *An Introduction to Theories of Personality*. New York, San Francisco, London: Academic Press (a subsidiary of Harcourt Brace Jovanovich, Publishers), 1980.

Kornfield, Jack. *A Path With Heart*. New York: Bantam Books, 1993.

Marova, Marova. *Open Mind*. Berkeley: Conari Press, 1996.

Moody, Harry and Carroll, David. *The Five Stages of the Soul*. New York: Anchor Books Doubleday, 1997.

Peter, Dr. Laurence. *Peter's Quotations*. New York: Bantam Books, 1977.

Pritchett, Priec. *Firing Up Commitment During Organizational Change, A Handbook for Managers*. Dallas: Pritchett & Associates, Inc., 1994.

Ray, Michael and Myers, Rochelle. *Creativity in Business*. New York: Doubleday, 1986.

Rose, Colin and Nicholl, Malcolm J. *Accelerated Learning for the 21st Century*. New York: Delacorte Press, 1997.

Sanders, Jr., Pete A. *Your Are Psychic*. New York: a Fawcett Columbine Book published by Ballantine Books, 1989.

Sloan, Price Stern . *The First Really Important Survey of American Habits*. Los Angeles, 1989.

Web Site
"Improving Workplace Dynamics"
http://www.human dynamics.com

Contact the author:
Human Dynamics, Inc.
P.O.Box 14402
Research Triangle Park, NC 27709-14402 ﹅
(919) 677-1452 or 1-888-525-7752
e-mail: hdinfo@human-dynamics.com

About the Author

Eileen Dowse is a motivational speaker, mediator, and educator with more than 20 years of business experience. Her highly acclaimed techniques have been successful in a variety of key industries ranging from high-tech, manufacturing, and non-profit to government agencies. Through her affiliation with Human Dynamics Inc., Eileen provides her clients with a variety of services, including educational programs, mediation sessions, conflict coaching, and employee relations consulting. She uses candid, on-target assessments and solution-generating methods to motivate clients to change behaviors. Eileen employs humor and magic to make workshop sessions entertaining.

Eileen has a Bachelor of Arts degree in Administrative Studies from the University of Winnipeg, a Graduate Certificate in Training and Development from North Carolina State University and is a trained mediator. She is a commentator for National Public Radio and produces and hosts the television show "Raleigh Talks."

As a professional, she is committed to building congruence within organizations and creating environments where all people can improve their workplace dynamics.

Index

G